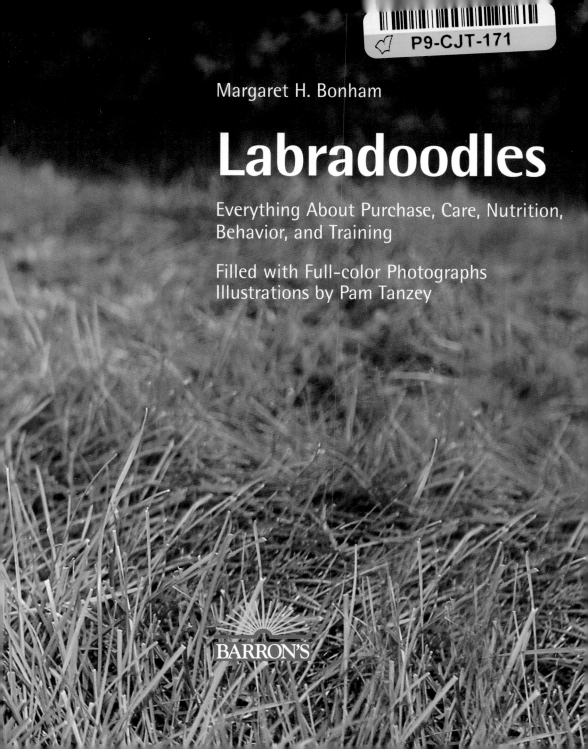

Margaret H. Bonham

Labradoodles

Everything About Purchase, Care, Nutrition, Behavior, and Training

Filled with Full-color Photographs
Illustrations by Pam Tanzey

BARRON'S

CONTENTS

WHAT IS A LABRADOODLE?

What is a Labradoodle, exactly? When we talk about Labradoodles, we're talking about a dog that has basically been separated into two types: the Australian Labradoodle and the Labradoodle. For simplicity's sake, I'm calling them both Labradoodles because the name is more or less synonymous with either.

No doubt, you're probably heard of the Labradoodle and the hype associated with them in the newspapers, on TV shows, and on the Internet. You're probably wondering what the fuss is about and why people are paying thousands of dollars for these dogs. Perhaps you've seen a Labradoodle in the flesh and liked their looks and temperament. Or maybe you're allergic to dogs and have heard that Labradoodles are hypoallergenic. Whatever the reason, you're looking into owning a Labradoodle.

Meet the Labradoodle

Labradoodles are dogs whose origins were crossbreeds between Labrador Retrievers and

Labradoodles are a blend of the best of Labrador Retrievers and Poodles.

Poodles. With Australian Labradoodles, the dogs are an F4 or greater, meaning that this is a fourth-generation Labradoodle or above.

Most Labradoodles are crossbred, meaning that they aren't a purebred in most respects. However see the section "Is the Labradoodle a Breed?" for further explanation.

Labradoodles come in three sizes: standard (21–24 inches), medium (17–20 inches), and mini (14–16 inches). All these measurements are height at shoulders. Labradoodles can be any variation of color of Labrador Retrievers or Poodles including chalk, gold, caramel, red, silver, black, blue, chocolate, café, and parchment.

The Labradoodle's coat can differ depending on the dog. There are three types of coat: fleece, wool, and haircoat. The latter being more like a Labrador Retriever's coat and less like a Poodle's coat and can shed profusely.

Labradoodles can come from crosses between Labrador Retrievers and Poodles like these Standard Poodles.

There's no doubt about it— Labradoodle puppies are adorable.

Personality

The Labradoodle's personality is very important because they are bred first and foremost to be pets and family companions. Labradoodles are smart and highly trainable, but like any dog, they need training and socialization. Because Labradoodles are clever, an untrained Labradoodle might cause problems for his owner.

Most Labradoodle breeders and owners will tell you that they're good with kids. This is a highly subjective statement because not all dogs of any breed or mixed breed are good with all kids. Any dog can bite, and leaving a kid alone with a dog completely unsupervised is asking for trouble.

F1 Versus Fn: First Generation Versus Multigenerational Dogs

When you start looking at Labradoodles, you may hear terms like F1, F2, and Fn. What these denote are generations from the original breeding of the first Labradoodle or foundation stock. Dogs who are F1 are a first cross of a Labrador Retriever and a Poodle. F2 is a dog whose parents were F1. Basically, F1 through F5 dogs are considered Labradoodles or foundation stock. Dogs who are F6 Labradoodles (with mostly Australian Labradoodle background) are considered Australian Labradoodles or purebreds.

There are other acronyms among breeders, but those are the basic ones. Breeders often talk about mixing back Poodle or Labrador Retriever into their foundation stock and use special

Grooming is a must with Labradoodles; be sure you're up to the task!

acronyms for that too. If you're not certain about what the acronyms do mean, you should ask the breeder to explain in terms of generations.

Which type of dog is better as a pet? Labradoodles and Australian Labradoodles are supposed to be bred for personality and health, so either will make fine pets.

Claims of Hypoallergenic Hair

One of the reasons you may be looking into buying a Labradoodle is the claim that they are hypoallergenic dogs. However, there is no such thing as a hypoallergenic dog. What spawns these claims is that many Labradoodles have Poodle-like, single coats that shed less than other dogs

(however, this isn't always so—many *do* shed).

Allergies are tricky things. Some people are not just allergic to the dog's hair or dander but to the dog's saliva. Some allergy sufferers can handle certain breeds over others, but it's not consistent.

Anecdotal evidence suggests that some allergy sufferers can deal with Labradoodles, but don't decide to buy a dog on that alone. It's better to talk with your allergist about how best to control your allergies around a dog and then to visit a Labradoodle breeder to see if you can tolerate them. Otherwise, you may pay a lot of money to purchase a dog whom you have to place if you can't tolerate him.

If you think you may be more tolerant of Labradoodles than other dogs, I recommend

Labradoodles can come in a variety of colors that exist in both foundation breeds.

visiting the home of a Labradoodle breeder and spending an afternoon with the dogs in their home environment. You'll learn quickly if you're going to have a reaction to these dogs, if your allergies respond quickly; otherwise, you may have to visit a few times to really decide if you're going to react.

A Brief History

The first Labradoodle was bred in 1989 by Wally Cochran in Australia for a person looking for a dog who would not affect his allergies. Cochran was looking for a smart dog who could work as an assistance dog, wouldn't shed much, and wouldn't trigger allergies. Twenty-nine of the first thirty-one Labradoodles bred became guide dogs, and although Cochran's promotion of these dogs triggered intense interest, most guide dog groups did not want crossbreeds.

Several major kennels such as Rutland Manor and Tegan Park worked toward establishing the Labradoodle from the original stock. Media reports quickly made the Labradoodle a success within the United States as buyers rushed to purchase this dog from breeders in Australia and also here in the United States.

Originally, the Labradoodle was a larger dog, being the product of Standard Poodles and Labrador Retrievers, but breeding with smaller Poodles has made three sizes of Labradoodles for pet owners.

Is the Labradoodle a Breed?

A few years ago, the answer would've been no—and in terms of origin dogs, the Labradoodle isn't a breed; it's a crossbreed. But at the time of this writing, the Australian Labradoodle is very close to being a purebred.

Color variations can occur even in the same color of Labradoodles.

When considering whether or not a particular dog is a purebred, I like to use the American Kennel Club's definition of a breed. A breed requires a national breed club that maintains a *standard* that is a guideline for what the breed needs to look like. The Australian Labradoodle Association of America and the International Australian Labradoodle Association do maintain a standard. They must also maintain a studbook, that is, a list of dogs who are bred, which these clubs do. They must also put on specialty dog shows, that is, conformation shows that determine which dogs are to standard with a minimum of 100 active households. For dogs to be considered purebred in the AKC's eyes, the dog must have a three-generation pedigree where all dogs within that breed are purebreds—the Australian Labradoodle qualifies in this case. The AKC requires that there must be more than 300 to 400 dogs in twenty or more states, which there are. Lastly, the AKC looks at the purpose of the dog and what the dog was bred to do.

Australian Labradoodles are not AKC registered, nor are there major breed registries who recognize them as a breed. However, the breed club is making a concerted effort toward making the Australian Labradoodle into a breed, which will someday be recognized by a reputable kennel club.

Smaller dogs, like these Toy Poodles, were used to reduce the size of the Standard Labradoodle.

The Labradoodle, that is, the F1–F3 crosses are *not* purebred. These are crossbred dogs and therefore cannot be considered purebred.

Why Do Labradoodles Cost So Much?

When you first look at the Labradoodle, you may be wondering why one costs hundreds or even thousands of dollars, especially when many are considered crossbred dogs. The answer is complex.

First, to be honest, the high cost of Labradoodles is largely associated with the

Labrador Retrievers are in the foundation stock of Labradoodles, lending part of its name.

demand and the popularity. Many people want these dogs, so breeders price their dogs on what the market will bear. These dogs have become popular due to television, newspapers, Internet, and radio, and some breeders have chosen to capitalize on this.

However, there's more to the cost than that. If you buy a puppy from a reputable breeder (see Chapters 2 and 3), you're paying for the cost of health tests and certifications, puppy care and costs associated with purchasing high-quality dogs. If you buy a puppy or dog from a reputable breeder, that breeder has quite a bit of time and money invested in the puppies, and, therefore, the cost is passed down to the buyer.

But just as not all breeders are good, not all Labradoodle breeders are good, so you'll need to do your homework to buy the best puppy you can. Price isn't always indicative of quality.

The Labradoodle in a Nutshell

The ideal Labradoodle is expressed in the Labradoodle standard from the International Australian Labradoodle Association. Basically, this is a guideline for breeders interested in producing the very best Labradoodle they possibly can. I've included some highlights from the standard here.

Size (at shoulders)

Standard (21–24 inches)
Medium (17–20 inches)
Mini (14–16 inches)

Coat

Coat should be 4–6 inches in length and may be either fleece, woolly, or haircoat. Fleece

Take me home!

is light and silky. Wool is less dense than lamb's wool. Haircoat is a shedding coat that is more like a Labrador Retriever's coat than a Poodle's coat.

Body

Body proportion should be 10 : 12 height to length ratio.

Color

Coat colors include chalk (white), cream (with hits of apricot or gold), gold, caramel, red, silver, black, blue, chocolate, café (milk chocolate to silver-beige), and parchment (creamy beige).

Nose colors include rose, black, and blue and should match the coat.

Temperament

They are playful, smart, nonaggressive, and highly trainable.

CHOOSING A LABRADOODLE

Just as not all places where you buy things are the same, not all places that offer Labradoodles are the same. When you look for your Labradoodle, you'll want to find the very best place to buy your Labradoodle. In this chapter, we explore where you should look for your Labradoodle and how to pick out the right Labradoodle for you.

So, now you know about Labradoodles, but is a Labradoodle right for you and your family? What's more, how do you go about finding the right Labradoodle? You're probably going to be paying a lot of money for your Labradoodle, so it makes sense that you should get the very best Labradoodle for your money.

Sanity Check: You Want a Dog, Don't You?

But before we get started on sources from which to buy your Labradoodle, and how to pick the best Labradoodle for your family, you must first ask yourself if a dog is really something you want. With all the hype about designer dogs and Labradoodles, the prices, and the promises, you must still remember that, in

Sharing your home with a Labradoodle can be a very rewarding experience.

the end, the Labradoodle is still a dog. That means once you have a Labradoodle, you have a ten to fifteen year commitment. You still have to housetrain (housebreak) your Labradoodle, train him, feed him, play with him, and basically rearrange your life to care for this dog for the next ten to fifteen years.

For many pet owners, this isn't a problem, as the inconvenience and commitment comes with the joy of companionship and having a great friend for many years. But for some new pet owners, the commitment and responsibility can be a bit of a shock. Dogs do not usually come trained, and you must spend a fair amount of time training, playing with, and socializing your Labradoodle.

Sources for Obtaining a Healthy Labradoodle

So, you know you want a Labradoodle, but where do you look for one? Do you visit the

If you want a healthy Labradoodle, buy only from a breeder who does health screenings and checks.

mall, look in the newspaper, or start going online and looking for dogs? Since you're likely to be spending a fair amount of money on a Labradoodle regardless of whether he is a puppy or adult, you'll want the healthiest dog with the best temperament. No one can fully guarantee how a dog will turn out, but buying a Labradoodle from a reputable or responsible breeder will give you the edge.

Nowadays, Labradoodle breeders are Internet savvy. The current breed associations for Labradoodles are the International Australian Labradoodle Association and the Australian Labradoodle

Association of America, which have breeder referrals online. This is a good place to start looking for your Labradoodle. The phone numbers for the organizations are in the back of the book if you don't have Internet access.

But just because the breeder is a member of a particular organization doesn't necessarily mean that they produce a quality Labradoodle. You will need to ask questions and determine if the breeder produces a quality Labradoodle.

So, what's the difference between getting a Labradoodle from a reputable breeder and getting one from a breeder who isn't? Despite the cost of a Labradoodle, the reputable Labradoodle breeder isn't in it for the money. The reputable Labradoodle breeder wants to produce a healthy Labradoodle who will make the perfect pet. These folks care about where their Labradoodle is going and whether you will be the right owner for their puppy. Responsible breeders will have health guarantees (within a certain time frame) and will do the right health screenings so their puppies are as healthy as possible.

What Screenings Are Really Needed?

Regardless of whether you believe that crossbreeds are healthier than purebreds, the reality is that all dogs are capable of inheriting certain genetic diseases. It comes from the fact that dog breeds aren't separate species, but part of *Canis lupus familiaris*—the dog.

Regardless of F1 or Fn breeding, all parents should be screened for hip problems such as hip dysplasia, either through PennHIP or the Orthopedic Foundation for Animals (OFA). Labrador Retrievers are prone to elbow dysplasia, so a PennHIP or OFA that includes elbows is very important too. Labrador Retrievers and Poodles share at least one type of hereditary eye disease called progressive retinal atropy (PRA), which leads to blindness. A certificate from Optigen and/or the Canine Eye Registry Foundation (CERF) is a must.

There are other hereditary diseases found either in Poodles or in Labrador Retrievers. Problems such as hereditary conditions that appear in one breed (i.e., sebaceous adenitis, a serious skin condition, on the Poodle side or tricuspid valve dysplasia, or TVD, a serious heart problem, on the Labrador Retriever side) can become a problem in Fn dogs who are not screened.

Check out the hereditary diseases in Chapter 5 for more information about what hereditary diseases can affect your Labradoodle.

Questions to Ask a Reputable Breeder

So, how do you determine if a breeder is reputable? It takes a lot of questions to determine if the breeder is one you wish to do business with. Here are the questions you should ask when looking for a reputable breeder:

✔ Are you a member of the International Australian Labradoodle Association or the Australian Labradoodle Association of America (or another Labradoodle club)? The answer should be yes in most cases—occasionally you'll find someone who isn't a member who breeds quality Labradoodles just the same.

✔ Why are you breeding these two Labradoodles? The answer should always be to produce quality puppies and to improve their breeding stock. The breeder may talk about a particular color

Don't forget that shelters and rescues can be great sources for Labradoodles.

combination or temperament she's looking for. That's okay, too.

✔ Are your prospective Labradoodle's parents screened for hereditary diseases? What proof does the breeder have that she has done these screenings? (See "What Screenings Are Really Needed?") She should be able to show you the original documents, not just copies. With OFA, you can actually check the names and numbers on their web site. The words "hips and eyes checked" is vague and means little; OFA and CERF certificates means the work has been done.

✔ Does the breeder have a contract? All breeders should have a contract stating the guarantee. The contract is your bill of sale.

✔ Does the breeder guarantee your Labradoodle's health for a certain amount of time? For example, most reputable breeders will guarantee hips and eyes for at least two years. If the dog is found to have a hereditary condition during that time, does the breeder offer a refund or replacement of the dog? (In many cases, owners become so attached to the current dog, that a replacement doesn't seem like a fair bargain). Look over the contact and understand what guarantees the breeder will give—and more importantly, what guarantees the breeder doesn't. Watch out for special caveats to the contract—you shouldn't have to feed a raw diet or limit your puppy's play to enforce the contract (although work such as agility, weight-pulling, or sledding may be included because these can stress a young dog).

It's wonderful having someone welcome you home.

Color isn't the only factor in choosing a Labradoodle. Health and personality are also very important.

✔ Does the breeder have health records on the Labradoodle? Did the breeder worm and vaccinate the Labradoodle appropriately?

✔ Does the breeder breed fewer than three litters a year? Any breeder, even one who does health checks, who breeds a large number of litters a year is most likely a puppy mill.

It's very hard for such an establishment to hand raise so many puppies or guarantee quality.

✔ How long has the breeder been owning and breeding Labradoodles? While Labradoodles are a relatively new crossbreed, the breeder should have some history with them.

A reputable breeder will screen for hip dysplasia, eye problems, and other potential health problems in your Labradoodle's parents. Ask for proof.

Should I Buy a Labradoodle, Sight Unseen?

Although the Labradoodle isn't a "rare breed," you may still find it difficult to find a Labradoodle from a reputable breeder close by or even in your region. Or you may be tempted to purchase a Labradoodle from another country. Should you do this?

Even though plenty of people have done this with success, you should always be cautious buying a dog from anyone, sight unseen. Quite often, you're looking at spending thousands of dollars—and that's not including shipping! There are many respectable breeders in other states and countries; nevertheless, Internet scams abound. You should never send money to a stranger for a dog you've never seen except in photos.

If you do decide that you want a dog from out of state, consider making a trip to visit the breeder and bring back your new pet, yourself. That way, you can meet the breeder, inspect the facilities, and make sure that the dog you're purchasing is the right dog for you.

✔ Will the breeder allow you to visit her facility? Are all the dogs friendly? Any dog who is aggressive should be a red flag to you. All dogs should be friendly and approachable, with the exception of a female who has had puppies because she may be protective.

✔ Does the breeder limit their breeding of dogs to one or two crossbreeds? (Or one of two breeds?) Breeders who breed many different crossbreeds may be doing this strictly for the money and not necessarily for producing healthy dogs.

✔ Does the breeder require the dogs to be spayed and neutered, either through contract or before you pick up the Labradoodle? This is

indicative of a breeder who understands that the dog is going to a pet home and wishes to prevent unwanted breedings.

✔ Does the breeder have referrals?

Looking to Adopt? Doodle Dogs Do Shelters

One place you may not think to look for a Labradoodle is a shelter or rescue. Because of the popularity of Labradoodles, there's a huge demand for Doodle dogs; consequently, many people are looking to make a quick buck. However, they soon find out that breeding

Getting a Labradoodle sight unseen may not be a good idea for the first-time Labradoodle buyer. There are usually breeders in the region that you can visit.

and selling dogs may not be as lucrative as they thought, and when they can't find homes for their dogs, they turn them into rescue, or worse, dump them in a shelter.

If you're not so worried about the pedigree and just want a Labradoodle without the designer dog price, check out the shelters in your area. These dogs aren't usually listed as a Labradoodle, but something along the lines of a Labrador mix, Poodle mix, or a Labrador Poodle cross.

In many of these shelter cases, you're most likely to get a dog who was not carefully bred, but in defense of the shelter dog, many of my own dogs have been from the shelter and made absolutely marvelous pets. Most had no health problems until they were much older and lived to ripe old ages past 13 years old. So, while careful breeding is important, you can still get a healthy dog from the shelter or rescue.

One word of warning, though. When you're looking for your Labradoodle, don't use the word "Labradoodle." Many shelter workers are averse to people who want a designer dog because of the hype, the crossbreeding, and the huge cost and that may be a red flag to them to not let you adopt the dog. It's better to look for a Poodle and Labrador Retriever cross rather than ask specifically for a Labradoodle. Looking for Poodle crosses is probably a safe bet.

Puppy or Adult?

Now, you have the task of deciding whether you want a puppy or adult Labradoodle. Most

TIP

What's the Youngest Age You Can Take a Puppy Home?

The youngest you should ever bring home a puppy is 8 weeks old. If you bring home a puppy younger than 8 weeks, he hasn't had the time to learn from his mother and siblings, and it can cause serious personality and behavioral problems later in life. If you bring a puppy home younger than 6 weeks, there's a chance he might not even be weaned yet.

Checking out a breeder will help you find a healthy and beautiful companion for many years to come.

people love puppies—and it's little wonder, puppies are so adorable. But puppies are a lot of work. They don't come housetrained and can be destructive. They need obedience training. Most Labradoodles are very trainable dogs, but training still takes time and effort. Plus, puppies grow up fast and quickly lose their charm.

Adult dogs are better for a person or family who doesn't have the time for a puppy. After their second birthday, they're usually a bit calmer. Adults are usually easier to housetrain (if they aren't already) and may know a few commands.

Some people are worried that adults won't "bond" to their new owners as readily as a puppy. This is nonsense. A Labradoodle is a very loving dog and will bond to you and your family, provided that you give him the love and attention he deserves.

So which is better, puppy or adult? It honestly depends on whether you have the time and the patience for a puppy. Adult dogs are great but can have bad habits from a former owner. Puppies may be a clean slate; however, they can learn bad habits very quickly if they are not trained correctly.

Male or Female?

In many cases, your Labradoodle will come to you already spayed or neutered, especially if you buy a puppy from a reputable breeder or if you adopt one from a shelter. Your Labradoodle should be loving and outgoing, regardless of whether it's male or female, so it's really a personal preference.

If you purchase an intact Labradoodle, you should always spay or neuter the dog for health and behavioral reasons. If you plan to breed your Labradoodle, consider the discussion in Chapter 5 on Spaying and Neutering. Twice a year for about three weeks, female Labradoodles go into estrus where you must make sure your Labradoodle does not breed with strays. Intact Labradoodles may show undesirable behavior such as urine marking, aggression (rare, but it can happen), attempts at escape to mate with other dogs, leg humping, and other unpleasant behaviors.

F1 or Fn?

When you're looking for a Labradoodle, you may hear a lot about various generational breedings. The most common are F1s and Fns. You may also discover various breedings that may be a Labradoodle bred back to a Labrador or a Poodle.

The International Australian Labradoodle Association defines a "purebred" Australian Labradoodle as being eight generations or more (with Australian Labradoodle primarily in the background). Dogs that are F1 to F6 generations are considered Foundation Australian Labradoodle stock.

By their definition, a Labradoodle is any dog that is a cross between a Poodle and a Labrador Retriever.

So, what makes the best pet? Honestly, it depends on what you are looking for. All Labradoodles and Australian Labradoodles can make wonderful pets. The issue you must decide is whether you want a dog who is more predictable in looks and temperament versus a dog who may have less chance of health problems. F1 dogs, that is, a cross between a Poodle and a Labrador Retriever *may* have fewer health issues than a dog who is multigenerational, but the breeder should screen for health problems, regardless. Dogs who are of multigenerations of Labradoodles (i.e., the Australian Labradoodle) will have a more consistent "look" and temperament.

For example, an F1 dog may or may not be low shedding, depending on how the genetics play out. An F8 dog is more likely to be low shedding if the breeder bred dogs for those traits. An F1 dog may look more like a Poodle or Labrador, or may be a total blend of the two. Dogs with many generations behind them will look more similar, and there will be fewer distinct Poodle or Labrador characteristics.

Understanding the Breeder Contract

Before you purchase your Labradoodle, the breeder should have furnished you with a con-

You should have a fenced-in yard or plan to walk your Labradoodle on a leash.

tract. This contract is your bill of sale. No matter what other papers your breeder may furnish, you should insist on a contract. The following points should be covered in the contract:

✔ The dog or puppy is yours to own. There is no shared ownership or co-ownership on the dog, unless this is something you agreed to in the beginning.

✔ You are not required to breed the dog to produce a puppy or puppies for the breeder to take back.

✔ There are specific health guarantees. These should at least include hips and eyes, but may include other guarantees such as thyroid, heart,

elbows, and skin conditions such as sebaceous adenitis and allergies.

✔ The breeder agrees to replace the dog or refund the purchase price (preferred) if a congenital or hereditary condition arises. A few really good breeders will offer to pay some portion of veterinary expenses.

✔ The breeder doesn't put bizarre limits on your Labradoodle's exercise or doesn't require you to feed a raw diet or other diet that might be impractical for you to feed.

✔ The breeder will agree to take the dog back *at any time of its life* if you no longer want him. (The breeder won't refund the money, however, if the dog is healthy or if the health problem is outside the guarantees.)

Labradoodles are smart and versatile.

✔ The breeder will require you to spay or neuter the Labradoodle, if she has not already had it done.

✔ The breeder will require that you treat the dog humanely and provide food, shelter, and proper attention.

✔ The breeder should require you to bring your Labradoodle to a veterinarian within the first week of ownership—this protects both you and the breeder because it ensures a healthy puppy.

If, for any reason, there is wording you do not understand in the contract, take the contract to a lawyer for interpretation.

When to Bring Your Labradoodle Home

The very best time to bring your Labradoodle home is when you have time to spend with him. A new dog or puppy in the house is a major disruption—even if you already have a pet. It's going to take several days for your new Labradoodle to get used to his new environment and people. He's going to probably fuss and cry the first few nights—in which case, you're not going to get much sleep.

For years, this author and others have railed against bringing puppies home around the holidays, but the reality is that if you're planning on having a quiet holiday at home, there's no good reason why you couldn't bring your Labradoodle home. I highly discourage giving pets as presents, but giving a pet to a close loved one (who wants the pet) can work out just fine, especially if that loved one has a say in choosing the pet. If your holidays are filled with visitors or you are going out of town, skip

Puppy or adult? Both have their advantages and disadvantages.

the holidays and plan a better time to bring your special puppy home.

Remember to never bring home a puppy younger than 8 weeks. After that, is just fine.

Choosing a Puppy

So, how do you choose a puppy? If you're purchasing a puppy from a reputable breeder, the breeder has been asking questions about you and your lifestyle. Don't take it as being nosy, she really wants to place the best puppy with you given your situation. Remember, the breeder

has had time to evaluate each puppy and can tell you a bit about their personalities. But, some breeders may allow you to choose your own puppy, if this is the case, you may be wondering how to choose the best puppy for you.

First, all puppies should be healthy. They should be neither pot-bellied nor thin, and have bright, clear eyes. They should be full of energy—unless they're asleep. They should have healthy, shiny coats and no diarrhea or other signs of sickness. If the puppies are sick, look elsewhere for your puppy. You don't need to have a sick puppy.

Should you get a first generation or multigeneration dog? It's really up to you and what you're looking for in a Labradoodle.

outgoing may be dominant, but not always. With the breeder's permission, try picking the puppy up and gently holding him in your arms on his back. If he fight and carries on without relaxing, he's probably too dominant. If he lays there without squirming at least a little or pees on himself, he may be too submissive. A good response is a puppy who may struggle a bit but who relaxes as you're rubbing his tummy.

Put the puppy down and clap your hands. You want the puppy to be interested in you; if he wanders off, he may be too independent.

Choosing an Adult

Choosing an adult is a bit easier because what you see is usually what you get. The adult you're looking for should be friendly and outgoing. Avoid any dog with signs of aggression, shyness, or hyperactivity (he should calm down after the initial greeting). If you can, put the dog on a leash and walk him around. If he knows commands, try getting him to focus on you and practice commands. A dog who is overly wary or shy isn't the dog for you.

Likewise, avoid very sick dogs or dogs who have serious health problems or personality problems. There are plenty of healthy dogs who are in need of homes, so don't fall for a hard-luck case. Treating dogs with serious health problems like heartworm and hip dysplasia can cost in the thousands of dollars.

Older dogs make good pets, so don't discount them. Many people think that dogs who are older than 3 years old are too old, but nothing could be further from the truth! A Labradoodle can easily live 13 years or more with good care, so even the so-called senior dogs over 6 can live between 7 to 9 or more years.

But what about personality? The best puppy in most circumstances is one who is neither dominant (pushy) nor submissive (shy). When being greeted by puppies, the boldest and most

Adults Labradoodles often make better pets than puppies. Check them out!

Ask the breeder, rescue organization, or shelter about the dog's past. You can often gain insight into a dog's personality by asking those people who are closest to him. They can usually tell you how the dog behaves on a daily basis. But regardless of what you are told, you and the Labradoodle should click and find that you have compatible personalities.

BRINGING YOUR LABRADOODLE HOME

Bringing home a Labradoodle can be a fun and rewarding time. Or, it can be a trying time. There are tricks in preparing for your Labradoodle and also in training your dog. By following the advice in this chapter, you can enjoy your Labradoodle more and have less stress on everyone.

So, now you have your Labradoodle, but what should you expect once you bring him home? How do you make your home safe and inviting to your Labradoodle? And how do you make the transition period for your Labradoodle easier on both you and your dog?

Where Is Your Labradoodle Going to Stay?

The first thing you need to decide is where your Labradoodle is going to stay. In almost every instance, your Labradoodle needs to be an indoor dog. Labradoodles are sociable dogs and were bred to be family companions. They are not intended to be relegated to the backyard and occasionally played with. If you're

You know you want me!
Bring me home!

looking for such a companion, the Labradoodle isn't for you.

So, your Labradoodle needs to be an inside-mostly dog, with occasional forays outside. But that outside must be safe, too. You can't expect your Labradoodle to know the boundaries of your yard. Nor can you expect the neighborhood dogs and kids to respect your yard either without a fence. So, it makes sense to have a fenced-in yard for your Labradoodle.

Where your Labradoodle sleeps is very important, too. He needs his own bed (sorry, kids!) and, for a while, that means a crate so he can learn the rules of the house. Remember, Labradoodles don't come housetrained, normally, so you're going to have to teach him it's not okay to eliminate on the floor. However, even though your Labradoodle needs his own bed, he needs to sleep with someone to whom you'd like him to bond, be it you or your kids.

Forays into the outside are fun; just make sure inside is where your Labradoodle sleeps.

You may wonder why your Labradoodle should not sleep with you. There are a number of reasons, but one of the most compelling is the occasional accident or sick time. Waking up

TIP

Quality Time While You Sleep

You may be surprised to learn that you can spend quality time while you sleep with your Labradoodle. It's true! Your Labradoodle will bond more closely with you if he sleeps in your room (but not on your bed!)

covered in vomit or urine is not fun. The second reason is up to debate with a dog as amiable as the Labradoodle, but I think the argument has merit. Dogs are pack animals, and some dogs can take the sleeping arrangements a little too seriously. When you sleep with a dog, you're more or less saying you're on an equal level. That's fine—if you don't mind getting bullied by your own dog. If you want to maintain a leader status, it's best to have your Labradoodle sleep in his own bed—and you in yours.

The basement, utility room, garage, and back-yard are definitely off-limits as sleeping places for your Labradoodle. Remember, these are sociable dogs, and they need attention. You're giving him a clear signal that you don't want

When He Won't Go to Sleep

There are many different high-tech type devices for helping your puppy sleep. One is Canine Lullabies, which mixes music with a heartbeat; the other is a product called Snuggle Puppies.

Some trainers swear by the ticking clock and hot water bottle in a blanket method. The idea is that a hot water bottle filled with warm water and wrapped in a blanket simulates your puppy's littermates, while the ticking of the clock imitates the mom's heartbeat. I've never tried this, so I don't know if it's really successful. Some people like playing light music to settle a puppy.

Do what works for you. If your puppy does wake up and fuss during the night, make sure that he doesn't have to go out to relieve himself.

It's really up to you if you want your Labradoodle on the furniture, but remember, he won't differentiate between patio furniture and your favorite chair.

him around when you make him sleep in a less-than ideal place.

How do you keep him from tearing things up and having an accident on the floor? You crate train your Labradoodle and put his crate in his designated room (see "Crate Training" later in this chapter).

Puppy (and Dog) Proofing

So, you've figured out the sleeping arrangements for your new pet, but have you dog-proofed your home? Dogs (and especially puppies) are masters at getting into things.

Look around your house. Some areas may be obvious; others will not be so obvious.

If there are areas you don't want your Labradoodle to get into, be sure that they're behind closed doors—and keep them closed at all times. Otherwise, invest in a good set of baby or pet gates that you can walk through but your Labradoodle can't.

Lastly, keep your Labradoodle out of areas that are inherently dangerous like the garage (always the threat of antifreeze poisoning) and areas with a pool.

Dangers abound in the backyard—be sure to dog-proof your yard to provide a safe place for your Labradoodle.

- Clothes, especially socks
- Dental floss—can become lodged in throat or intestine
- Electrical cords
- Garbage pails
- Glass knickknacks
- Grapes—toxic to some dogs
- Houseplants
- Irons and ironing tables
- Kitchen knives
- Medications—including ibuprofen, acetaminophen, and aspirin—and vitamins.
- Nuts (Certain types of nuts such as macadamia nuts can cause paralysis.)
- Onions—can cause anemia
- Paper shredders
- Pennies—can cause "penny poisoning" due to the zinc content
- Pens, paper, and other small items that may be chewed or swallowed
- Plates and glasses—can be knocked over
- Scented soaps, potpourri, scented plug-ins, and air fresheners
- Sewing needles and craft kits
- Shampoo, conditioner, and mouthwash
- Suntan lotion
- Toothpaste—extremely toxic to dogs

House

Your house is probably going to be the main place your Labradoodle will live. Look through each of the rooms for items your Labradoodle might be able to chew and swallow. Look not only at his height level but also at what he can put his paws up on. Here's a partial list of things you need to put away and keep out of reach:

- Alcohol
- Bathroom and shower cleaners
- Candles
- Children's toys, especially those with small pieces that can be chewed off or swallowed
- Chocolate—extremely toxic to dogs (Dark chocolate is more poisonous than milk chocolate.)

Yard

Your yard is probably the other place your Labradoodle will be in regularly. Be sure that you have a fence and a gate. In most cases, I recommend a 6-foot high fence if the dog is big. If you have a smaller Labradoodle, you can probably get by with a 3- or 4-foot fence.

However, there are still dangers inside your yard for you to be aware of:

• Cocoa mulch—Some places now sell this type of mulch. Unfortunately, it is both attractive and dangerous to dogs because it is made from cocoa bean shells and has a high amount of theobromine (the substance in chocolate that is poisonous to dogs).

• High decks—Dog can accidentally jump from them.

• Lawn and garden chemicals—These chemicals can be absorbed through paw pads or licked off fur.

• Mushrooms and fungi—Many are toxic or even deadly.

• Sharp edging—This trim can cut paws.

• Stones—Many dogs love to eat small rocks and gravel that can lodge in intestines.

• Swimming pools—Dogs can get in and accidentally drown.

• Toxic plants—These plants are too numerous to list but include evergreen plants such as holly and pods from the black locust tree. Con-

Your fence should be dig-proof, jump-proof, and climb-proof to foil a Houdini-Labradoodle.

tact your local poison control center or state agricultural office for a listing of possible poisonous plants in your area.

Going to the Veterinarian

Before you bring your Labradoodle home, you should have made an appointment with a veterinarian to have your new family member

Feed your Labradoodle a balanced diet for boundless energy and good health.

checked within the first week after you bring him home. There are several reasons for doing this:

✔ It ensures that your Labradoodle is healthy coming from the breeder.

✔ It ensures that your Labradoodle is up to date on all his vaccinations and dewormings.

✔ It starts your Labradoodle off right with a health check and enables your veterinarian to establish a good working relationship with you when it comes to your Labradoodle's health.

✔ It enables you to ask questions about your Labradoodle concerning health care, training, and nutrition.

Your veterinarian will know what vaccines to give your Labradoodle. If your Labradoodle is a puppy, he may need more than one series of vaccinations. Ask your veterinarian about the right times for vaccinating your Labradoodle. In many cases, vets will send reminder cards that will let you know when you need to set appointments for important routine care such as heartworm testing, vaccinations, and health checks.

Many breeders require in their contracts that you bring your Labradoodle to the veterinarian within a certain time period (within 72 hours to one week) to ensure that the puppy was healthy when it left the breeders. Be sure to check your contract and bring your Labradoodle to the veterinarian within that time frame.

Puppy Nutrition

You may be surprised to learn that nutrition is a bit of a controversial subject nowadays. There are a plethora of homemade diets (both cooked and raw) and various dog foods out there; however, most advocates will tell you that their diet is the best.

The reality is that unless you know what you're doing and have a diet analyzed, homemade and raw diets can be risky due to potential deficiencies and bacteria. They can be costly and somewhat inconvenient to prepare as well. If you choose to do the homemade or raw diets, be sure to discuss them with your veterinarian and perhaps a veterinary nutritionist to determine if you're meeting all the nutritional requirements your Labradoodle needs.

If you're not interested in raw or homemade diets, there are plenty of good puppy foods available. In most cases, skip the grocery store and bargain brands because they tend to be chock-full of sugar, salt, artificial colors, flavors, and fillers that do nothing nutritionally. Although grocery stores occasionally carry premium brands, the best place to look for puppy food is a pet supply store or even a feed store. Look for a premium dog food formulated according to AAFCO (American Association of Feed Control Officials) guidelines as complete and balanced for growing puppies or for all life stages.

The basic rules for choosing a puppy food are these:

✔ The puppy food must be complete and balanced and have some statement of meeting or exceeding AAFCO guidelines for formulation or in feeding trials. It must be formulated either for all life stages or for growth.

✔ The puppy food should be a premium brand. "Premium" is only a marketing term; nevertheless, you need to look for a food that is highly digestible. (See Chapter 6 for more information).

✔ You should be able to buy the puppy food at more than one retailer near you.

✔ Your puppy likes the food.

Look at the dog food's label for feeding guidelines. Most dog food have some sort of feeding guidelines for size and age of your puppy. If it doesn't, ask your veterinarian what would be an appropriate amount for your puppy. More on dog food and nutrition in Chapter Six.

Getting Through the First Few Days (and Nights)

If you're a new pet owner, owning a puppy is probably going to try you for the first few days. You'll be surprised at how much attention the little guy needs and how much cleanup you're going to have to perform. Puppies get into

You'll need to put your Labradoodle on a schedule in order to housetrain him.

everything, and you're bound to discover that your Labradoodle is no exception. While some pet owners may have angel puppies, you may be pulling your hair out over your "devil dog."

First, be aware that your Labradoodle is new to this situation. No matter how often you tell him to not have an accident on the carpet, he probably is going to have one. Puppies can't "hold it" and don't housetrain quickly, except in the most unusual circumstances. (See "Crate Training" and "HOW-TO: Housetraining" later in this chapter.)

Play with your puppy right before bed and be sure to take him outside to relieve himself right before putting him in his crate.

Many new puppy owners like to cordon off a couple of rooms where their puppy can safely play and it isn't a big deal if they have an accident there. A puppy will get into everything and anything, and most puppies love to explore by chewing things. Even if you provide the right assortment of toys, I've discovered that puppies will chew inappropriate items all the time.

The best way to combat puppy rambunctiousness is to simply tire your puppy out. No, I'm not talking 5-mile hikes here; I'm talking about playing with your puppy until he is played out. Puppies play quite a bit and then drop off for a quick nap to recharge themselves (lucky you!). If you have a puppy who is misbehaving, chances are it's because he's wide awake and ready to play.

But how do you get a good night's sleep? The first few nights, your Labradoodle may howl and cry for a short while or for almost all night. There are several tricks for getting him to go to sleep, but the best way is to play with him before bedtime until he becomes tired. Make sure he relieves himself outdoors before putting him to bed at night.

Crate Training

You may have heard about crate training but may not think this is something you should do because it looks cruel or because you've had a bad experience with trying to train a dog to it in the past. The truth is, crate training isn't cruel. It works because dogs have a natural

CHECKLIST

Main Things to Remember

✔ Choose a time when your Labradoodle is tired. After exercising or play is a good time.

✔ Feed your Labradoodle in his crate. Give him his toys and treats there. Let him know that this is a special place.

✔ Make your dog's experience in the crate as inviting and positive as possible.

✔ Start in small time increments. Try a few minutes at first, and gradually build up time spent in the crate.

✔ Don't leave a young puppy (younger than 6 months) in a crate longer than 4 hours, and don't leave an adult in a crate longer than 9 hours.

✔ Only open the crate after your Labradoodle has stopped fussing. You want to reward good behavior—not bad behavior.

denning instinct. Remember that the dog's ancestor is the wolf. A dog has many of the same instincts as his ancestor—and one of them is to live in a den, which is a fancy term for a hole in the ground. Most dogs feel safe and secure in an enclosed area—my own dogs will hide under a piece of furniture during a thunderstorm. So, a crate simply harkens back to the time when dogs felt secure in a den.

The crate needs to be just big enough for him to stand up and turn around in and not much more. If you have a puppy, you'll probably have to get a puppy crate first and switch out to a full-size crate when he gets bigger.

You don't want a full-size crate for a puppy because he can have accidents and avoid them. More on this in the housetraining section later in this chapter.

How you crate train is very important. You can't just stick your dog in there and expect him to accept it, especially if he has nothing interesting in there. Most likely if you put a puppy who has never been crate-trained in a crate, he's likely to think you don't want to be with him and will fuss and fume.

So, start crate training first by tossing treats into the crate and then let him go into it and explore. Put a nice comfy bed and some toys in it. Feed him in it. Before you put him in the crate and close the door, be sure you have exercised your Labradoodle and have taken him outside to relieve himself, so he's a little tired. Put him in the crate with some food, treats, or chews and shut the door. If he's tired, he might just fall right to sleep.

If he's fussy, wait until he quiets down before letting him back out of the crate. You may have to try this several times until he learns to accept the crate quietly. Sometimes playing soothing music or having a special toy, might help.

Basic House Manners

How your Labradoodle behaves is pretty much up to you. Before you bring your Labradoodle into your home, you need to decide what behaviors are okay and what aren't. For example, some people don't want their Labradoodles to climb up on the furniture, jump up on them, or enter certain rooms. Start thinking about what behavior is acceptable because once you allow a certain behavior, it's hard to stop.

For example, let's say you don't mind your Labradoodle lying on the ratty old sofa. But you may care if you replace the old sofa with an expensive sofa. Your Labradoodle won't care that you paid $5000 for that new sofa, so be sure you really want him on *any* sofa when you let him climb up on it.

TIP

Car Temperatures Can Soar
Although you probably already know this, it bears repeating: Never leave a dog in the car on a warm day, even with the windows down. The car temperature can soar rapidly and can cause overheating.

House manners and your Labradoodle are strictly up to you. Labradoodles are pretty smart, so training them to behave shouldn't be an issue if you're consistent.

Also, be aware that certain behaviors can be cute as a puppy and downright dangerous as an adult. It may be cute for your Labradoodle puppy to jump up on you, but it may be a different story when your adult Labradoodle jumps up and knocks over grandma. Mouthing is cute as a puppy, but it can turn to biting if it isn't discouraged early.

The main thing with house manners is consistency. Don't allow one behavior one day and then ban it the next. What frequently happens is that one person enforces the command and another family member does not. Make certain that *everyone* knows and enforces the behaviors you want, otherwise you may have one confused pup.

Traveling with Your Labradoodle

Occasionally, you'll have to travel with your Labradoodle—whether it's to the veterinarian, to the park, or on vacation. Assuming they go places they like, most dogs ride well in the car. If all you do is drive your Labradoodle to the veterinarian, then he's going to hate riding in the car.

Keep your Labradoodle restrained in the car. That means he should be in a crate while you drive. If he's old enough and well-behaved enough, you can opt for a seat belt restraint system to keep him safe in an accident.

Never, for any reason, have your Labradoodle ride in an open truck bed. Dogs can be thrown from the truck in an accident or even a sudden stop.

Travel or Board?

You've got a big trip planned, but you don't know if you should bring your Labradoodle with you. Maybe it's a vacation. Maybe you're going on a business trip and would like to take your Labradoodle along. Whatever the reason, you're wondering if you should take your Labradoodle with you.

You should take your Labradoodle with you if
• You're moving cross-country.
• Your Labradoodle is housetrained and knows basic obedience.
• Your Labradoodle travels well.
• The place you're going has activities for you to do with your Labradoodle.
• You're able to have your Labradoodle with you most of the time on this vacation.

You should board your Labradoodle if
• The place you're staying isn't dog-friendly.
• You aren't going to be spending much time with your Labradoodle.
• Your Labradoodle isn't going to be able to go places with you while you're there.
• The hotels or other lodging doesn't accept pets.

• Your Labradoodle hates to travel or gets carsick.
• Your Labradoodle is destructive or isn't housetrained.

Looking for a Good Boarding Kennel or Facility

If you decide to board your Labradoodle, it's important that the boarding facility is top-notch. After all, these are the people who will take care of your dog while you're on vacation.

Your dog-owning friends may recommend someone with whom you can board your Labradoodle. Often these are excellent recommendations because they've trusted their dogs to these facilities. Your veterinarian may also board dogs or have recommendations. Contact the American Boarding Kennel Association for kennels in your area if you have no other recommendations. Be sure to visit the facility to make sure it's clean and in good repair. Be sure you know what vaccines they require, and make sure your Labradoodle is up-to-date on vaccinations.

An alternative to boarding is to hire a pet sitter, but don't count on a friend or relative to do it, unless they're really good and have experience with it. Ask your veterinarian, dog trainer, and other pet-owning friends who does pet sitting in your area. Often, vet techs or trainers are looking for other income and double as pet sitters.

Contact Pet Sitters International or the National Association of Professional Pet Sitters for pet sitters in your area. Regardless of who you get, be sure that they're bonded and insured and check references—these are the people you're letting into your house.

Housetraining, or "house-breaking" as it is commonly called, is basically teaching your Labradoodle to eliminate outside instead of inside. When you are first house-training your Labradoodle, you need to stick to a schedule. This schedule is very important because your Labradoodle will rely on it until he is housetrained. Even then, he will expect to go out to eliminate during these times:

✔ When he first wakes up
✔ Anytime after he eats and drinks
✔ Before you go to school or work
✔ Midday, around lunchtime
✔ When you come home from school or work
✔ After he plays or exercises vigorously
✔ Before bedtime

That may sound like a lot, but remember, small puppies and dogs who aren't house-trained, may not have the bladder control (or capacity) necessary to "hold it" much longer. By putting your Labradoodle on a schedule, he learns that he can expect to eliminate during these times and thus wait for it.

Be aware that housetraining can go very slowly or very fast, depending on the dog, his age, and other factors.

For Puppies

Housetraining puppies can be a bit frustrating at first. For one thing, you can think that they might have figured it out one day, and the next day, they forget all about it. With some puppies, it can take six months to a year for them to be truly reliable.

✔ When your puppy first wakes up or after he eats, drinks, or plays or when you come home or before you go to bed, whisk him outside and put him in the area where you wish him to eliminate. Give him a chance to eliminate—most puppies will use this time to investigate and play—be patient!
✔ When your puppy elimi-nates outside, praise him!
✔ If he doesn't, you may have to play with him a bit or run around the yard a bit. He'll eventually squat and eliminate. Praise him.
✔ If your puppy was paper-trained, putting a small piece of newspaper out where you want him to go may entice him to eliminate.
✔ Other methods to get your puppy to eliminate outside is to put his feces in the area he needs to go and put down housetraining pads sold in some stores. When he elimi-nates, again, praise him.
✔ Only have your puppy loose in your home when you can watch him. Otherwise, he needs to be crated.
✔ It can take a long time for a puppy to become reliably housetrained. Expect relapses up to one year.
✔ Never make a puppy younger than 6 months "hold it" for more than 4 hours,

Crate training your Labradoodle will help reduce destructiveness and will aid in housetraining.

with the exception of overnight. Even so, if he whines at night, you will need to let him out.

✔ Follow the training plan as outlined in the preceding section.

Be very patient with your puppy. Most puppies really aren't housetrained for several months, even when you are vigilant.

For Older Dogs

Housetraining an older dog is usually a bit easier. If your older Labradoodle isn't housetrained, it usually takes a lot less time to housetrain him than it would to train a puppy. You'll need to crate train him, just as you would a puppy. However, you can expect to have a shorter time to housetrain him. Keep these things in mind:

✔ When your adult first wakes up or after he eats, drinks, or plays or when you come home or before you go to bed, whisk him outside and put him in the area where you wish him to eliminate. Give him a chance to eliminate—be patient!

✔ When your adult eliminates outside, praise him!

✔ Only have your dog loose in your home when you can watch him. Otherwise, he needs to be crated.

✔ Never make an adult "hold it" for more than 9 hours.

✔ Follow the training plan as outlined in the preceding section.

✔ Lapses in housetraining may signal health problems. Take him to the veterinarian to get checked out.

Accidents

What should you do if your Labradoodle has an accident inside the house? Even though you may be tempted to "rub his nose in it" or swat him on the butt with a rolled-up newspaper,

A household answer to accidents: soap and water to clean the mess, followed by white vinegar and water to counteract the smell.

that's not very effective (in fact, most trainers think this is cruel). Instead, you need to be vigilant and watch for signs when your Labradoodle is getting ready to eliminate. Sniffing around and squatting are definite signs, as is circling. If you catch him in mid-elimination, rush him outside to finish his business.

Now onto cleaning up the mess. Most cleaners are ammonia-based and although they may give a piney-fresh scent, it won't fool your Labradoodle. In fact, they actually enhance the urine smell since urine is ammonia-based. And if you don't get the urine or feces out, it will just tempt your Labradoodle to eliminate there again. So, what do you do?

There are basically two methods for cleaning up accidents. One is to use a prepared enzymatic cleaner to clean up accidents, available in any pet store. Clean up what you can with paper towels and then follow up with the enzymatic solution (follow the directions on the label). The other method is to use soap and water to clean the mess and then follow it up with white vinegar and water. The vinegar will counteract the smell.

BASIC OBEDIENCE

You now have your Labradoodle. He's cute, but he's a handful. So, you've started thinking about taking him to obedience or maybe training him yourself. This chapter covers the basics of, well, basic obedience. It also covers what you may or may not know about training dogs.

Do-It-Yourself or Hire a Pro?

Should you train your Labradoodle yourself or should you hire a professional trainer to help you train him? It's pretty amazing that people think they are experts when it comes to dog training, despite the fact they've never successfully trained a dog in their lives. These people wouldn't think anything of hiring a mechanic to work on their car or buying an airplane ticket to fly somewhere (instead of learning to fly and flying their own airplane) or hire a plumber for a clogged line. But somehow, people think they should know how to train dogs properly.

If you've gotten this far, you know where I'm going with this. Unless you're a dog trainer, you can't really expect to know how to train

Your Labradoodle is ready to learn!

your Labradoodle properly. Yes, there are instructions in this chapter for how to do-it-yourself, but it's a little like doing surgery on yourself via a correspondence course. It can be messy and painful at times, and I don't think you'd particularly like the outcome. But if you're thinking you'd like to give it a try, go for it. Just remember that your mistakes may take a long time to correct that would've been avoided if you had decided to use a professional trainer in the first place.

Finding a Professional Trainer

Finding a professional trainer is relatively easy. You'll need to look for a trainer who teaches primarily positive training techniques. There are several reasons for it, but the compelling reason is that it's kinder to your Labradoodle. Labradoodles can be very sensitive, and

Teaching clicker is the fun way to train. Your Labradoodle will be focused on what is coming next.

Why Clicker Train?

Clicker training is a way to teach your Labradoodle in a way he understands. By clicking on the behavior you want, you're telling your Labradoodle: "You got it right! Such a good dog!"

Clicker training is a method of positive reinforcement—that means that you offer rewards for a job well done. You don't yell at, spank, or jerk around your Labradoodle to get his attention. Instead, you use something that motivates him such as treats or food—or, on occasion, a toy.

choosing a method that rewards instead of punishes often works well. So, how do you find one? You can ask your veterinarian, who may have affiliations with certain training facilities, or, if your friends and neighbors take their dogs to a particular trainer and you like the results, check him or her out. If you can't find a positive trainer, try the Association for Pet Dog Trainers (see Information section) and see if there is a trainer in your area.

Plan to visit the trainer during a class without your dog to watch how he or she trains. The trainer should be delighted to have an observer. If the trainer is worried you'll "steal her secrets," consider looking elsewhere. Watch and see how the trainer trains. Is she effective? Does she use gentle methods? Does she train the owners to train their dogs?

When you settle on a trainer, be aware that you're there to learn how to train your dog. You shouldn't hand off your dog for training because that does nothing to strengthen your bond between you and your dog.

Lastly, remember cost isn't everything. Cheap, cookie-cutter classes from pet stores or community colleges may or may not work for you. Problems such as aggression and serious behavior problems may be out of their league, so be sure to ask, especially if there's a particular problem you need to address.

Basic Obedience Commands

There are basic commands that every Labradoodle should know. Those include: walk

Click the clicker to mark what you want your dog to do.

After clicking, give him a treat.

nicely on leash, heel, sit, stay, down, and come. To teach these commands, I recommend using a training technique known as "clicker training." Clicker training is a simple way to teach your Labradoodle that he's doing something you want him to do.

People often say that their dog isn't food-motivated, but he loves steak, cheese, popcorn, or whatever. Yes, you can use those treats as long as you keep them very small because you're going to be using a lot of them. So, look for something your dog really loves, whether it's food or toys, and use those as clicker treats.

Teaching the Clicker

The clicker is simply a way to "mark" desirable behavior. In truth, you don't need an actual clicker to do this, but it tends to be more effective than saying "good dog" or using something else. The reason why clickers work so well is that, first, they make a definitive sound that is different than anything else your dog might hear. Second, the clicker works better in terms of timing. You can click on a good behavior faster than you can say "good dog!"

Starting with the clicker is pretty easy. You need a bag of treats cut into tiny portions (you'll be using a lot) and a clicker.

1. When your Labradoodle is a little hungry, you'll want to click the clicker and then give him a treat. Do this several times until when you click the clicker, he awaits the treat. Please note, you may have to do several short sessions of this before he "gets it."

You can teach your Labradoodle to walk nicely on leash—without a tug of war!

sometimes he must wait for the treat. Vary the times between the clicks and treats.

4. Keep these lessons short and fun. Don't make a lesson last any longer than 5–15 minutes.

If, at any time, you get frustrated, take a break and play with your Labradoodle. Or put up the clicker and treats and give your Labradoodle a break the rest of the day.

Now, you have a "marker" for determining what good behavior is. You see, when you click for a behavior (whether it's good or not), your Labradoodle will expect a treat. Your Labradoodle will associate his current action with the click and, subsequently, the treat. He will try to obtain the treat again by performing the behavior again. If you click and treat (C&T) that behavior, he's going to figure out that doing that behavior causes the click and, therefore, the treat.

Walk Nicely on Leash

Once your Labradoodle learns that the clicker means a treat, he's now ready to learn how to walk on a leash. What you'll need is a treat pouch, your clicker, and your dog's leash to get going. You can use either a training collar or his regular flat (buckle-type) collar, provided it is tight enough on his neck that he can't pull his head through it.

1. Clip the leash on his collar or training collar and go outside. He may be very excited and may whirl around you or try to pull you or may simply wait to see what you're doing.

2. Get his attention by showing him a treat and bring the treat up to your nose.

3. Click and treat when he makes eye contact.

4. Start walking. If he forges ahead, use a treat to lure him back to eye contact. C&T.

2. Once your Labradoodle is used to hearing a clicker and then receiving the treat, click and then toss the treat a little ways away from you. If he doesn't go after the treat, show it to him. Do this several times so your Labradoodle gets the idea that the treat doesn't have to come from your hand. Remember, this may take several sessions before he learns this.

3. Once your Labradoodle learns this, click and then wait a few seconds before you give him a treat. With this lesson, he learns that

5. If he keeps a slack leash going in the right direction, C&T.

6. At first, you'll be giving out lots of clicks and treats to get your dog to stop pulling or at least going in the right direction. Don't worry, you'll be weaning him off the treats.

7. Once your dog is reliably walking on leash without pulling, decrease the number of clicks and treats slowly over time. Where you may have been treating him once every minute, try once every two minutes, until he's reliable with that. Continue to lengthen the amount of time, once your Labradoodle is successful at walking on leash.

8. If, at any time, he starts pulling again, get his attention and then C&T for a loose lead. You will have to work with him longer with more C&Ts until he becomes completely reliable on leash.

Heel is a very important command that needs to be taught.

TIP

Fading the Clicker

Eventually, you're not going to want to use the clicker. Once your Labradoodle is consistent on a particular command, you can slowly fade out the clicker by not clicking for every time your Labradoodle performs a command. For example, with heel, you may only choose to click on the sits when you stop. Then you can fade the click out by clicking on every *other* sit, and then clicking at the end of the heel session, and so on. Instead of clicking, substitute praise with occasional C&T as a reminder.

Heel

Heel (and heel position) is a very important command for your Labradoodle to learn. Although you might not think that teaching your Labradoodle to walk on your left side is important, consider that you may have to do this on a crowded, busy street or in areas where you may need more control over your Labradoodle. The heel position is the place where you'll be teaching your Labradoodle the basics for sit, down, and stay. It's another command that your Labradoodle should learn.

Getting your Labradoodle to sit isn't hard.

The heel position is along your left side. Ideally, he should be standing or sitting when in heel position.

1. Clip the leash on his collar or training collar and go someplace where he can learn. It's ideal if he knows the sit command as well. You can work on both together.

2. Get his attention by showing him a treat and bring the treat up to your nose.

3. Click and treat (C&T) when he makes eye contact.

4. Now use a treat to lure him to your left side. C&T when he goes to your left side. It's okay at this point, if he isn't perfect.

5. When he leaves your left side, lure him back, and C&T.

6. Once he has the idea that your left side is a good side and he wants to hang out there, start C&T for him standing straight ahead on your left side and not just for being on your left side.

7. Once he has a good idea of this, start walking. If he stays by your side, C&T. Otherwise, use a treat to lure him back to your side, and C&T when he does.

8. You need to practice this a while and then start adding turns. If he's confused and gets out of position, use the treat to lure him back, and C&T.

9. As your Labradoodle now learns to walk beside you in heel, you can start using the word "heel" so he can associate it with what he is doing.

10. Now, stop. Your Labradoodle should stop with you. If he knows "sit," tell him to sit. Otherwise, make him sit as per the instructions for sit. When you start walking again, pat your leg and tell him "heel." If he's reluctant, tell him he's a good dog and lure him forward with a treat. C&T when he returns to heel position. Have him sit every time you stop.

11. Keep practicing heel until he becomes reliable with the clicker. Then, slowly reduce the number of C&T until he is heeling without the clicker.

Sit

Sit is an important command for your Labradoodle to learn. It's good if you need to have control over your dog or need him to settle down just a bit. Sit is a very easy command to teach.

1. Clip a leash to your dog's collar.

2. Get his attention by showing him a treat and bring the treat up to your nose.

3. Click and treat when he makes eye contact.

4. If he knows heel, put him in heel position.

5. Now take a treat and hold it just above his nose.

Show him the treat and bring it over his head to get him to sit.

6. Move the treat backward so that he must try to follow the treat with his nose. He may instinctively sit to get it. C&T.

7. If he just backs up, either have him stand next to a wall with his rear end close to the wall and try step 5 or when you move the treat backward, apply *gentle* pressure on his rear so he starts to sit. C&T.

8. You can also C&T whenever you see him sitting.

9. Once he understands sit, you can then add the command, "sit" to the action.

10. As he gets better with sit, start reducing the numbers of clicks and treats until he's reliably sitting without the clicker.

Showing off—"Look! I can sit!"

Stay

Stay is also a useful command, however, it can be somewhat difficult for young dogs to learn because they're so rambunctious. However, stay can actually save your Labradoodle's life, especially around busy streets. Your Labradoodle can learn stand–stay, sit–stay, and down–stay.

1. Clip a leash to your Labradoodle's collar.

2. Put your Labradoodle in heel position. C&T.

Stay is sometimes tough to teach. Increase time or distance but not both while your Labradoodle is learning.

3. Now you can either have your Labradoodle in sit, down, or simply standing. C&T if you put your Labradoodle in sit or down.

4. Now, give the command "stay" and keep your hand flat and open and push it toward his nose in a "halt" signal as you step forward and turn around so you face him.

5. He may come with you. Stop and gently put him back in place. Repeat the signal and command. Be patient. You may have to do this several times.

6. The moment he stays in his position, C&T. It's okay if he breaks the stay after the C&T for now. Use the release word "OK" to signal that it's done.

7. Practice this until he's confidently staying with you in front of him.

8. Now, lengthen the time he must stay. If he breaks early, shorten the time for C&T, so

you have a success. Continue to train at that time until he's reliable.

9. Continue to lengthen the time a little at a time, building on success. Always C&T at the end of the time.

10. If, for any reason, he breaks a stay, put him back in stay and try again with a short time. C&T.

11. Then, lengthen the distance you are away from your Labradoodle. Instead of being right in front of him, take two steps back and have him stay for 5 seconds. C&T if he stays. Otherwise, return him to his stay position and try again.

12. Once you have consistent success, step out to the length of the leash (about 5–6 feet), and practice short stays there. Then, once he is confident with that, you can increase the time or distance, but not both.

Eventually, you'll want to teach your Labradoodle to stay off leash. When you do, choose an enclosed place such as a fenced-in backyard. You will want to start just as if you had never taught him stay, but without the leash; that is, start your stay facing him and gradually increase the time and distance with each success.

Down

Down is also an important command for your Labradoodle to learn. Like sit, it's good if you need to have control over your dog or need him to settle down just a bit. Down requires you to have taught sit.

1. Clip a leash to your dog's collar.

2. Get his attention by showing him a treat and bring the treat up to your nose.

3. Click and treat when he makes eye contact.

4. Have your Labradoodle sit. C&T.

To teach down, start with sit.

Bring a treat toward your Labradoodle's chest. You can also show him where you want him to go.

5. Hold a treat at nose level and bring it downward toward your Labradoodle's chest. He should lower himself for the treat, C&T.

6. If he does not lower his head, you may have to gently press on his shoulders or tug gently at his collar. Do *not* do this roughly, as this can be construed as an aggressive behavior. C&T.

7. Practice down several times. Add the word "down" as a command when he learns the behavior.

A nice down!

Bringing a treat to the floor will help teach the puppy the down command.

With clicker training, you can even teach tricks, like "shake."

Come

Come is possibly the most important command for your Labradoodle to know. Think about it—if he doesn't come when you call, you could lose your Labradoodle if he accidentally got out of the house or, worse yet, wandered into a busy street! So, come is very important.

You should already be rewarding your Labradoodle for coming to his name. Praise and C&T are everything he needs when you call to him.

1. Get the clicker and treats out. Your Labradoodle will probably come running toward you. C&T.

2. Use his name with the command such as, "Rusty, come!" and C&T when he does.

3. Then, clip a leash to his collar and put him in stay. Stand the length of the leash (about 6 feet) and release him with an "OK" and then "Rusty, come!" When he comes, C&T. If he doesn't come, show him the treat, and when he comes, C&T.

4. Work on this several times until he's reliably coming to you at this distance.

5. Get a retractable leash that's very long, and clip it onto your Labradoodle's collar. Put him in a sit–stay and walk out to the end of the retractable leash. Release him and call him to you, letting the retractable leash retract as he does. C&T. Again, if he is confused or distracted, show him the treat, and C&T when he comes.

6. When he's reliable, you can try the come command off leash. Just be certain to do this in an enclosed area so if he decides not to come, he can't run away. A backyard or fully fenced-in empty ballpark might work. Start with short distances such as 6 feet or less. If he bolts or doesn't come, show him the treat and lure him

TIP

Important!
Never punish your Labradoodle after you call him to you, no matter what he's done. Always reward and praise him for coming to you.

back. C&T. *Do not* punish him for not coming to you. Always reward him, even if you have to chase him down. If he does bolt, start his training at the beginning.

The Canine Good Citizen Test

You may be surprised that your Labradoodle can earn a title from the American Kennel Club called the Canine Good Citizen or CGC. Any dog can get his CGC certificate by demonstrating good manners and basic obedience. This test includes:

1. Accepting a friendly stranger
2. Sitting politely for petting
3. Appearance and grooming
4. Walking on a loose lead
5. Walking through a crowd
6. Sitting on command and staying in place
7. Coming when called
8. Reacting to another dog
9. Reacting to distraction
10. Reacting to supervised separation

Each of these tests prove that your Labradoodle is good with people and other dogs, thus making him the ideal canine good citizen. You can learn more about the CGC program

through the American Kennel Club (see Information section).

Problem Labradoodles

No matter how wonderful Labradoodles are, sometimes you end up with one who becomes a problem. Maybe it's because you let him get away with a bit of bad behavior "just this once." Whatever the reason, you may have a badly behaved dog.

So, what do you do? First, don't look at the behavior as being spiteful or malicious. Dogs don't feel spite. Instead, consider one of three possibilities:

1. Your Labradoodle may have a medical condition. This is especially true if he never did this behavior before. Regardless of whether you think the behavior is, well, behavioral, have him thoroughly checked over by a veterinarian and talk with the veterinarian about the problem.

2. Your Labradoodle is too young to expect consistently good behavior yet. Puppies younger than 6 months are bound to make lots of mistakes—and puppies younger than a year can still be inconsistent.

3. Your Labradoodle never learned good behavior.

Reasons 1 and 2 are not reasons to think that your Labradoodle exhibits bad behavior. Reason 1 requires medical attention, and Reason 2 requires basic training and patience. If you have an adult Labradoodle who hasn't completely learned to be housetrained, for example, you're likely to have accidents from time to time.

The best way to stop bad behavior is to keep it from happening in the first place. That means always be consistent with your Labradoodle's training and be sure to enforce all rules.

LABRADOODLE HEALTH

In this chapter, you'll learn the answers to whether Labradoodles are really healthier than other dogs and you need to worry about the hereditary health problems that owners of purebred dogs do. You'll learn about the basics for keeping your Labradoodle healthy and also what to do in an emergency.

Your Labradoodle is a special dog to you. This is why it's so important to maintain his health for a good, long life. But your Labradoodle can't always tell you when he's sick. And your Labradoodle's veterinarian doesn't see him enough to catch a problem when it's starting. It's up to you to recognize problems before they happen.

Are Labradoodles Healthier Than Other Dogs?

The question of whether Labradoodles are healthier than purebred or other dogs is a largely debatable and complex question, mainly because the answer is "it depends." Labradoodles, as you know from Chapter 1, are crossbreeds; that is, they're made up of two purebreds: the Labrador Retriever and the Poodle (Standard and Minia-

Labradoodles can make good family pets.

ture). There are several lines of Labradoodles, including the Australian Labradoodle, but they come from basically two purebreds, whether single generation or multiple generations. No matter how different the Labs and Poodles look, they're not separate species—deep down inside they're still dogs.

According to an article in *Science Magazine* (May 2004) on the genetic structure of purebred dogs, genetic mapping seems to indicate that most breeds were developed within the last 200 years. The genome mapping suggests that dogs can be clustered into six types, but basically, they're all dogs, meaning that each breed probably has attributes and genetic problems within their genes that other breeds do.

So the talk of "hybrid vigor" isn't helpful here. A dog is a dog and can carry the same doggie hereditary diseases regardless of whether he is a mixed breed, crossbred, or purebred. It's been this author's experience

Your veterinarian will be your partner in maintaining your Labradoodle's health.

Poodle to a dysplastic Labrador Retriever will most likely result is dysplastic puppies (as may breeding two carriers of the disease). PennHIP results also confirm what OFA does, and they allow Labradoodles registered there (see sidebar on *PennHIP Statistics*).

However, there *may* be some hereditary conditions that affect only certain breeds. In this instance, obtaining an F1 (that is, a first generation) dog may be a better bet, *if* the offending gene isn't dominant. But obtaining an F2 (second generation) or subsequent generational breeding will nullify the gains you may receive with an F1 dog. Basically, with any limited gene pool, there's the tendency for negative traits to reappear, especially if one or more ancestors are doubled up. At the same time, even if you use dogs who are technically unrelated, there are still possibilities for hereditary diseases given that many diseases exist in different breeds. The author's own experience is that mixed breeds are often no healthier than purebreeds and in many instances may be actually worse if no genetic screening is done. (See Chapter 1 on how recessive and dominant genes are inherited.)

A better determination for your Labradoodle's health comes from whether the breeder did the correct screening for hereditary diseases. If your Labradoodle's breeder did the proper testing, there's a better chance of his being healthy. However, genetic testing and screening isn't a panacea. Plenty of hereditary and congenital problems crop up that can't be tested for. Likewise, testing isn't foolproof and occasionally a dog with a hereditary disease slips through.

with crossbred and mixed breeds that hereditary diseases can crop up just as easily in these dogs as they can in purebreds. Diseases caused by the same genes are so widespread throughout purebreds and mixed breeds that putting two dogs from different breeds together isn't going to mitigate the disease.

For example, according to the Orthopedic Foundation for Animals (OFA), 12.7 percent of Poodles and 12.4 percent of Labrador Retrievers out of all those reported were dysplastic. (The numbers are most likely higher given that many breeders don't report dysplastic dogs and that OFA is a voluntary registry.) Hip dysplasia affects all breeds, and breeding a dyplastic

TIP

No Guarantee on Health

Don't expect to have a healthy Labradoodle just because he's a crossbred. The breeder should have done the proper genetic testing and health screenings on the parents *before* they were bred.

The Orthopedic Foundation for Animals, PennHIP, Canine Eye Registry Foundation (CERF), Optigen, and Vetgen are all legitimate health registries in the United States. If you receive your Labradoodle from Australia or another part of the world, the dog should have hips, elbows, and eyes registered with the British Veterinary Association/Kennel Club (BVA/KC), Health Scheme or the Australian Veterinary Association and Australian National Kennel Council (AVA/ANKC).

The other part of the equation is how well you care for your Labradoodle. All the best genetics in the world won't count for much if you don't take proper care of your dog. That means providing good nutrition (Chapter 6), practicing good grooming (Chapter 7), and eliminating parasites (this chapter and Chapter 7). You can make the difference in your Labradoodle's health.

Choosing a Veterinarian

The first step to ensuring your Labradoodle's health is to choose a good veterinarian. However, choosing your Labradoodle's veterinarian may be a little daunting. After all, this is the

PennHip Statistics

As you will recall from earlier chapters, PennHIP does a genetic registry for hips as well and Labradoodles are registered with PennHIP. According to PennHIP, if the Distraction Index (DI) is greater than 0.3, dogs may develop DJD or degenerative joint disease (such as hip dysplasia). Not all dogs with a DI greater than 0.3 will develop DJD, but the greater the number, the more likely the dog will have this disease.

PennHIP results show that DJD as it relates to the DI number is breed-specific, meaning that some breeds may have higher DI numbers and still not get DJD. Even so, the samplings with PennHIP are small and don't necessarily give an accurate number on how many Labradoodles may get DJD. In 2005, the semiannual results showed the 75th percentile of Labradoodles as having 0.39 DI—very much above the 0.3 limit. The 50th percentile (i.e., the average) is at 0.50, which is very similar to the Labrador Retriever's and Standard Poodle's 50th percentile, both at 0.48. In other words, the Labradoodle is shown to have as much (if not more) propensity toward DJD as either purebred that makes up this crossbreed.

Like OFA, PennHIP is a voluntary registry and so doesn't give a truly accurate measurement of DJD among breeds and crosses because it's more likely that reputable breeders register their dogs and others won't. Therefore, you can assume that hip dysplasia is more common than either registry indicates.

person to whom you entrust your Labradoodle's health. But, you're in luck! There are plenty of great veterinarians out there, and one may be just around the corner. But how do you find out who's good?

Word of mouth is the best way to find out who's a good veterinarian. Ask your dog-owning friends and coworkers where they take their pets. Chances are they'll give a glowing recommendation for their veterinarian or a veterinarian not too far from you. If they're not too forthcoming with names of veterinarians they really like, contact your Labradoodle's breeder and ask her whom she might recommend. She may not be in the same state, but she may know people in your area to whom she has sold puppies and can ask them who they use. You can also ask dog groomers and dog trainers whom they would recommend.

Labradoodles can have the same hereditary diseases as many purebreds.

If you can't get any good recommendations, you may have to resort to opening up the phone book and looking for a veterinarian in your area. While you're looking, think about the types of services you're looking for in a veterinarian. Not all veterinarians are the same, so consider the following checklist:

✔ What are the office hours of the clinic?
✔ How many veterinarians are working at the clinic? (Standard clinics have anywhere from one to five veterinarians; large clinics and animal hospitals usually have a large staff.)
✔ Does the clinic handle emergencies after hours? Is there an on-call veterinarian available?
✔ Does the clinic have specialists? (If your Labradoodle has a condition that needs treating, having a specialist at the same facility is a good idea.)
✔ Does the clinic provide other services such as boarding, grooming, or training?
✔ Is this a low-cost clinic? (Some clinics provide low-cost treatment for routine care such as spay/neuter and vaccinations. However, to keep costs lower, their services are limited.)
✔ Does the veterinarian offer a multipet discount?
✔ Does the clinic accept pet health insurance?
✔ Does the vet offer holistic treatments?
✔ Is the clinic a mobile clinic or does the veterinarian make house calls?
✔ Is this a hospital or a university clinic with access to the latest treatments and diagnostics?
✔ Has the veterinarian treated Labradoodles before?

You'll have to decide what's important to you when it comes to selecting a veterinarian. For example, office hours and the ability to contact your veterinarian in an emergency might be very important to you, whereas having a groomer on-staff might not.

Call the veterinarians' offices to check out each veterinarian. Then, once you have narrowed your choices, call each and schedule a visit where you can come by and see the facility. It's not a good idea to drop by unannounced because you might come by during an emergency or a very busy time where they wouldn't be able to answer your questions.

When you visit the veterinarian, you should be comfortable with what you see. The clinic should be clean and in good shape; the veterinarian and staff should be welcoming and courteous. Watch how they handle the animals—are they gentle and caring? They should be disinfecting exam tables between pets and keeping cages and kennels clean.

Not all veterinarians will work for you and your Labradoodle. Even if your friends give glowing recommendations about a particular veterinarian, trust your instincts. If you don't like the veterinarian, chances are you're not likely to listen to his recommendations. There are plenty of other veterinarians available, and you should be able to find one whom you and your Labradoodle will like.

The Health Check

One way you can take an active part in maintaining your Labradoodle's good health is to do a complete health check, preferably every

Be sure to perform a health check on your Labradoodle at least once a week.

TIP

When to Perform Health Check

If you're having problems keeping your Labradoodle still for a health check, try doing the health check when he's a little tired—maybe in the afternoon after he has played or before bedtime.

day, but at least once a week to determine if something is wrong with your Labradoodle.

The health check provides several benefits:

✔ It provides extra social time that you might not normally spend with your Labradoodle.

✔ It familiarizes you with your Labradoodle's anatomy—what is normal and what is not.

✔ It will alert you to potential health problems before they become big.

✔ It will teach your Labradoodle to accept handling even in tender or ticklish areas.

You can do a full health check anytime when you have a few minutes to spend with your

CHECKLIST

What to Regularly Check For

When beginning the health check, be sure to perform it the same way each time in order to get into a routine. That way, you're sure not to skip over anything. If you find something that looks or feels strange, try looking for it on the opposite side of the body. Normal features are usually symmetrical, but if you aren't sure what's normal, ask your veterinarian.

If you find something abnormal, it's time to schedule a visit with the veterinarian. He can determine the proper treatment.

✔ Head—Look for lumps and bumps that might indicate tumors. Look for rashes, red areas, and scaly skin.

• Ears—Is there is a foul odor or a grainy, waxy substance in the ear? Is the ear reddened or inflamed? Any of these could be signs of ear mites or an ear infection.

• Eyes—Are the eyes clear and bright with no signs of redness? There should be no excessive discharge or weeping. Likewise, there should be no pus or yellow or green discharge. Dogs don't cry, so anything beyond a small amount of tearing may indicate an infection or a foreign body in the eye.

• Nose—The nose should be moist and cool to the touch. There shouldn't be a discharge. Your dog's nose shouldn't be scaly or raw either. Any of these signs or excessive sneezing indicates a possible problem.

• Mouth—The mouth should be sweet smelling and free of "doggy breath." Bad breath indicates a possible health problem. The teeth should be clean and white—free from plaque and tartar. (If they are discolored, it's time for a dental cleaning by your veterinarian!) The gums should be pink and healthy—not red or inflamed. Look for broken teeth or teeth that have turned brown, indicating a possible tooth problem. Look inside for strange growths and bumps—these can indicate oral tumors or abscesses. If your Labradoodle is older than 6 months, look for puppy teeth that haven't come out yet. Learn all about basic dental care and exams in Chapter 7.

✔ Skin and coat—Look (and feel) over your Labradoodle's entire body for lumps and bumps. Sores, tender red spots, and lumps (especially those that are warm to the touch) are not normal. Look for fleas and ticks as well. Grainy red, brown, or black pieces of dirt that turn red when wet are signs of flea infestation. See tips for grooming your Labradoodle in Chapter 7.

✔ Legs and feet—Feel down your dog's legs for unusual lumps and bumps—or any sign of tenderness. If you feel a lump, check the other leg to see if it's symmetrical, in other words it is present in the same place on both legs. Move the leg through its natural range of motion (do not force it into odd positions). The movement should be fluid, and there should be no clicks or pops. Examine your

Labradoodle's feet too. Look at the top, bottom, and in between the toes. Check for broken nails. Look for redness, lumps and sore or cut pads. Redness of the hairs around the feet indicates excessive licking and may indicate allergies.

✔ Back and abdomen—Feel along your Labradoodle's spine and ribs. You should be able to feel his ribs without searching—if you can't, your Labradoodle may be obese. Feel for lumps and bumps in these areas, and look for fleas and flea droppings especially along the base of the tail and the abdomen. If your Labradoodle is hunched up or shows tenderness

around the lower back where the kidneys are, this may be a sign of a more serious condition.

✔ Sexual organs and anus—If your Labradoodle is female and spayed, there should be no discharge coming from her sexual organs. If she is intact, there should only be a light discharge during her estrus or heat (any other discharge is a serious problem). Males can have a small discharge but nothing that suggests an infection. The anus should not be irritated nor should there be growths around it. If you see something that looks like grains of rice near your dog's anus, he may have a case of tapeworm infestation.

Labradoodle. Many owners like to perform the health check while they're grooming their dogs (See Chapter 7), but you can do a quick health check anytime.

Go slowly and gently the first few times you perform a health check, especially if your Labradoodle isn't used to being handled quite so much. It doesn't really matter where you start the health check as long as your Labradoodle is comfortable with it.

Vaccinations

Vaccinations protect your Labradoodle from deadly diseases such as rabies, parvovirus, and distemper. Young puppies and elderly dogs are more susceptible to diseases than adult dogs, but any dog may contract and die from these diseases. If you purchased your Labradoodle puppy from a reputable breeder, she should have her first series of vaccinations. If your Labradoodle is an adult, the breeder should

have vaccinated her against all diseases. The breeder should provide you with a vaccination record indicating the date of the vaccinations and the type of vaccination given.

Your Labradoodle will need a series of vaccinations to prevent many contagious and dangerous diseases that can seriously affect your Labradoodle's health and in some cases, even kill him. These vaccinations protect against diseases such as distemper, parvovirus, adenovirus 2, parainfluenza, and rabies.

At one time, it was common practice to vaccinate dogs for all possible diseases available to vaccinate against. However, current veterinary practice has changed with the appearance of autoimmune diseases that are caused by reactions to overvaccinating. Many veterinarians still vaccinate annually; however, many try to evaluate risks and vaccinate accordingly. Not everyone agrees what is the best way to protect a puppy or dog from diseases, so this remains a highly controversial topic.

Vaccinations—The Technical Stuff

Vaccinations work by introducing a small amount of the organism in the form of killed, modified live, or recombinant vaccines. In killed vaccines, the dangerous organism is completely killed and then introduced into the dog. In modified live vaccines, the deadly organism is genetically altered to remove its dangerous components, but the organism is still able to reproduce. The dog develops antibodies against the killed or modified organism that will protect the dog against the disease. Killed vaccines are generally safer than those that use modified live organisms, but vaccines made with modified live organisms are usually more effective because the body must produce more antibodies to combat the "infection." Recombinant vaccines come in two different varieties: genetic deleted recombinant and live agent recombinant. In genetic deleted recombinant vaccines, the organisms are modified by selectively removing genetic code for virulence factors, thus making the

disease harmless. In live agent recombinant vaccines, the genetic code of the disease is inserted into a "carrier" that passes the disease's genetic code on. Both of these vaccines appear to be more effective than the modified live or killed vaccines. Because vaccinations rely on a healthy immune system, you should never vaccinate a sick dog.

Puppies are normally protected by their mother's colostrum, the milk the dam secretes during the first 24 hours after the puppies are born. The colostrum is rich with maternal antibodies that will protect the puppies until they are about 5 to 15 weeks old. After that time, the puppies are susceptible to diseases. Vaccinating a puppy before the maternal antibodies fade will not protect the puppy. The maternal antibodies will override any vaccinations. The idea behind vaccinating puppies every few weeks is to hit the window after the maternal antibodies fade but before the puppies are exposed to the disease.

Colorado State University (CSU) and other veterinary colleges have developed a vaccination protocol for dogs that recommends a three-shot series for puppies (distemper, parvovirus, adenovirus 2, and parainfluenza) and, after 16 weeks, a rabies vaccination. They recommend a booster shot 1 year later and vaccinations every 3 years after that. CSU recommends other vaccinations or more frequent vaccinations for dogs and puppies who are more at-risk. For example, if kennel cough is a big problem in your area, vaccinating your puppy against *Bordetella bronchiseptica* may be a good idea.

The best thing to do is talk with your veterinarian about vaccinations and what your Labradoodle really needs. He or she can give you good advice in protecting your dog against dangerous diseases.

Spaying and Neutering— A Healthy Reason

If you've been a pet owner for any length of time, you've probably heard you should spay and neuter your Labradoodle to prevent unwanted litters. If you bought your Labradoodle from a reputable breeder or a shelter, she may have already had your puppy spayed or neutered. Many reputable Labradoodle breeders often make certain that their puppies have been spayed or neutered before they leave for their new homes.

Spaying is removing the uterus and ovaries from the female dog, and neutering involves removing the testicles from the male dog. A competent veterinarian can spay or neuter your Labradoodle.

But if you haven't spayed or neutered your Labradoodle yet, you may be wondering why you should. After all, you probably spent a lot of money on this dog. Believe it or not, spaying and neutering is *healthy* for your Labradoodle. You can help prevent or even eliminate certain health problems. Let's take a look at some good reasons to spay/neuter your Labradoodle:

✔ It reduces or eliminates certain types of tumors and cancers in your dog. In males, it eliminates the chance of testicular cancer and greatly reduces anal tumors. In females, it eliminates the chance of ovarian and uterine cancers and greatly reduces breast cancer, if done before the dog's second estrus or heat.

✔ It prevents unwanted pregnancies and makes you a responsible pet owner.

✔ It helps curb aggression in both males and (arguably) females.

✔ It eliminates the urge to roam to look for mates.

✔ It helps focus your Labradoodle on you and not on sexual urges.

✔ It eliminates the heat cycle—you don't have to worry about the mess or about strange dogs coming around.

✔ It virtually eliminates pyometra, a deadly condition which can kill your female dog.

What about the stories you hear about dogs becoming fat and lazy? Dogs become fat and

Follow your veterinarian's advice concerning vaccinations. Your puppy will need to be protected against deadly diseases.

lazy when their owners overfeed them, not because they're spayed or neutered. In fact, most pet owners find that their dogs simply become better pets when they're spayed or neutered.

Possible Hereditary and Congenital Diseases

As you know from an earlier discussion in this chapter, your Labradoodle can only be as healthy as his care and his genetics. So, what kind of hereditary diseases can your Labradoodle have? Basically anything that the Poodle or

Spaying and neutering is a healthy thing to do, as well as the right thing to do.

the Labrador Retriever might have. Your Labradoodle is only as good as his ancestors—the genetic makeup of his parents is vitally important. So, if your Labradoodle's breeder screened the parents for various diseases, chances are pretty good that your Labradoodle doesn't have these conditions.

Allergies—A Potential Hereditary Condition

Allergies are something that is on the rise in both purebreds and mixed breeds, and Labradoodles are no exception. There's no genetic testing and no registry that compiles dogs with allergies. Allergies are the reaction

of a dog's body to a substance. The offending substance that causes a dog's allergies may be ingested, inhaled, or come into contact on the skin.

Many dog allergies manifest themselves in the skin and coat. In an ingestion allergy, the dog may show sensitivity to certain types of food and may break out in an itchy rash. In contact allergies, the dog starts having a reaction to a substance put on his skin (like a type of shampoo) or brushed against (like pollen). In inhalation allergies, the dog inhales something that bothers him and causes a reaction (sneezing, snorting, runny eyes, etc.). In contact and inhalation allergies, removing all of the offend-

(See more on hypoallergenic diets in Chapter 6.) Depending on your Labradoodle's reaction to these diets, you can either keep your Labradoodle on this diet or try introducing different foods he used to eat to see if he has a reaction.

Dogs who show severe allergies should not be bred in case the allergy is hereditary.

Elbow Dysplasia—A Potential Genetic Disease in Labradoodles

Elbow dysplasia (ED) is a type of polygenic (multi-gene) hereditary disease that affects the elbows. Dogs who are born with this disease have malformed elbow joints. This disease can be painful and may need surgery, anti-inflammatories, or special nutritional supplements (called nutriceuticals) to mitigate the effects of this disease.

Dogs who have this disease shouldn't be bred. OFA has a registry for elbow dysplasia. The only way to confirm elbow dysplasia is through X-rays (radiographs).

OFA shows Labrador Retrievers as the 24th worst in breeds with ED, having 11.5 percent dysplastic dogs, and Poodles as the 62nd worst breed with only 1.8 percent of cases of dysplasia registered. Be aware that because OFA is voluntary, the numbers are likely to be much higher. Even so, ED is more likely to occur in an Fn dog than an F1 dog, but the potential is there.

Hereditary Eye Diseases

There are a number of hereditary eye diseases that your Labradoodle can suffer. Some hereditary eye diseases, such as *Prcd*-PRA are the same genes in Poodles (Miniature and Toy) as they are in Labrador Retrievers and thus can cause the disease if two dogs with the recessive genes exist.

=== TIP ===

Allergy or Intolerance?

When people talk about allergies, sometimes they mean intolerances. For example, some people are lactose intolerant, they can't digest milk sugars. (Dogs can be lactose intolerant too!) Dogs can be intolerant to certain foods, and they will cause digestive upsets. In a food allergy, the problem often manifests itself in problems with the skin and fur.

---

ing substance (e.g., washing it from your Labradoodle's fur), may be all that you have to do. If the reaction is serious (hives, anaphylactic shock), seek immediate veterinary attention.

Dogs can also get a condition known as flea allergy dermatitis (FAD) where the dog becomes allergic to flea bites. (See Chapter 7 for more information.) Dogs can also have rare allergic reactions to vaccinations, which can cause hives and/or swelling of the face or, in extremely rare instances, anaphylactic shock. (Both require immediate veterinary attention.)

Some allergies, especially food allergies, which are becoming more prevalent in many different breeds, are hereditary and can be quite frustrating to diagnose. If your Labradoodle has skin problems, they could very well be food allergies. Excessive licking of the foot can be an indication of an allergy as well. Talk with your veterinarian. If the veterinarian suspects that your Labradoodle has food allergies or dietary intolerances, he or she may put your dog on a hypoallergenic diet.

Having your puppy and his parents screened for hereditary diseases will help ensure a long and healthy life.

in the case of juvenile cataracts, they can spontaneously reabsorb. Cataracts can be screened through CERF.

• Entropion and ectropion—These are both hereditary conditions that affect the eyelids. Entropion is a painful condition where the eyelid curls in and presses your dog's eyelashes against his eye. Ectropion is a sagging lower eyelid that exposes the eye to the environment. Both can be corrected with surgery. Mild ectropion can occasionally be remedied with special eye drops from your veterinarian. Both conditions can be screened through CERF.

• Progressive retinal atrophy (PRA, *Prcd*-PRA)—This is a hereditary disease that causes blindness in dogs. There is more than one type of PRA in dogs, but it appears that one of the common forms of PRA is a type called *Prcd*-PRA. This disease causes the retina to degenerate, eventually leading to blindness. There's no treatment for PRA at this time; however, we know that *Prcd*-PRA is caused by a recessive gene. CERF will screen for dogs who have PRA, but it is Optigen who can screen for the actual recessive gene through a special genetic test.

Diagnosing an eye condition can be a bit tricky. Sometimes a regular veterinarian can diagnose eye conditions, but many eye conditions need to be evaluated by a veterinary ophthalmologist.

Your Labradoodle may show little or no outward signs of blindness (dogs compensate for it well, especially if they're among familiar surroundings such as their backyard or inside their home). However, your Labradoodle may bump

There are two ways to screen for eye problems. One is through the Canine Eye Registration Foundation and the other is through Optigen. (See Chapter 2 for information on genetic tests and on CERF and Optigen.) CERF isn't foolproof because it requires the condition to happen before the exam. Let's look at some of the eye conditions your Labradoodle might have.

• Cataracts—This condition is caused by cloudiness in the eye lens. It can be partial or total (total causes blindness). Juvenile cataracts are hereditary. Surgery can sometimes fix these, or

into things when in a new environment or if you add something new (like a piece of new furniture in a new spot). Night blindness is often a precursor to these problems, but you might overlook it if you're not watchful.

Heart Problems

Cardiac problems seem to occur more in the Labrador Retriever than in the Poodle, but an F1 cross is no guarantee that a dominant hereditary cardiac problem couldn't manifest itself in a Labradoodle and an Fn cross could produce problems coming from recessive genes. Problems such as tricuspid valve dysplasia (TVD), which causes a deformed heart, can be mild to severe, and may show up in Labradoodle lines that have not had parents screened through the OFA.

Some heart problems can be diagnosed through a normal veterinarian, but certain conditions may need a cardiac specialist for both diagnosis and treatment.

Hip Dysplasia

Hip dysplasia (HD) shows up in nearly every breed including the Poodle and the Labrador Retriever, and consequently the Labradoodle. It is a hereditary disease that can be very debilitating, and no amount of good nutrition will correct a dog who is born with this disease. Hip dysplasia is caused by the malformation of the hip joint. It can be extremely painful, depending on the severity. In mild cases, anti-inflammatories and nutriceuticals may help mitigate the effects. In many cases, expensive surgery is required to fix the problem, and in extreme cases, the only kind thing to do is to euthanize the dog.

This is why it is very important to make sure your Labradoodle's parents are screened for hip

All Labradoodle puppies are cute. Make sure yours is healthy, too.

dysplasia either through OFA or PennHIP. The only way to diagnose hip dysplasia is through X-rays (radiographs).

Dogs can occasionally have environmentally or nutritionally induced dysplasia due to injury (extreme overexercising) or an imbalance of calcium. Not forcing your puppy to do repetitive jumping (agility) or pulling (such as weight-pulling or sledding) and feeding a balanced diet will prevent this.

Luxating Patella

Luxating patella is a painful condition that is either hereditary or congenital. Sometimes called a "slipped stifle," this condition is where the knee slips out of place. It can be corrected only through surgery. Both Poodles and Labrador Retrievers rank high on the list of dogs OFA sees with patella problems; therefore, Labradoodles are at risk for this disease.

Labrador Retrievers are the fifth worst breed for luxating patella with 17.9 percent of dogs showing this disease. Poodles (all sizes) are shown as sixteenth worst with 6.4 percent of dogs evaluated having luxating patella. (Remember that this is a voluntary registry and the numbers are most likely greater.)

Sebaceous adenitis affects mostly Poodles, so an Fn Labradoodle might be susceptible to it.

A veterinarian can diagnose this condition by manipulating the joint. (Do not attempt to do this as you can severely injure your dog).

Sebaceous Adenitis

Poodles are the number one dog with issues when it comes to the hereditary disease known as sebaceous adenitis. This condition causes hair loss and seborrhea. It can be very painful and can erupt into secondary infections. According to the Poodle Club of America, it's estimated that 50 percent of all Standard Poodles are carriers for this serious disease.

It can be treated with Accutane, corticosteroids, and a variety of anti-seborrhea drugs and shampoos available from your veterinarian, depending on how serious the condition is. Labradoodles may be affected with sebaceous adenitis from their Poodle side. Because this is primarily a Poodle condition, Fn dogs are primarily susceptible to this disease. The OFA maintains a database of dogs with sebaceous adenitis. If you suspect your Labradoodle has sebaceous adenitis, your veterinarian will need to diagnose it with a skin biopsy.

Internal Parasites

There are lots of nasty creepy-crawlies out there to make your Labradoodle very sick. In some cases, these internal parasites can actually kill your pet if left untreated. Let's look at the major internal parasites.

Worms

Worms are nasty parasites that can seriously affect your Labradoodle's health. They often take away vital nutrition that your puppy or dog needs to thrive. In some infestations,

Worms don't care how cute your Labradoodle is. Be sure to have your veterinarian check for worms so your Labradoodle can be healthy.

worms can actually kill a dog. Whipworms and hookworms, for example, can cause severe anemia. Roundworms can take away enough nutrition to actually kill a puppy.

Reputable breeders will worm their puppies (and the mother) to keep the infestation at bay. Even so, some puppies do have roundworms and may need follow-up treatments.

But there's more to worms than just the danger to your Labradoodle's health—some of these worms can actually affect *you*. Certain worms, like roundworms, hookworms, and even tapeworms, can be transmitted to people (especially children) who eat soil or who have contact with infected feces and do not wash their hands before eating.

The following are common worms you may see with your Labradoodle:
• Roundworms (*Toxocara canis*) are the most common worms that infest dogs. These worms can infest the intestines, stomach, and lungs and feed off vital nutrition your dog needs. Your Labradoodle can contract them through ingesting contaminated soil or through his mother before he was born or while nursing. You can occasionally see roundworms in your dog's stools or he may cough one up.
• Hookworms (*Ancylostoma caninum*) are worms that feed off blood in the small intestine. Your Labradoodle can contract them through penetration of the skin or through his mother before he was born or while nursing.

Many puppies are born with worms, so be sure the breeder has dewormed the pups before you bring yours home.

• Tapeworms (*Dipylidium caninum*) are worms that live in the intestines. These worms are usually contracted through fleas (dog bites and swallows flea), but occasionally a dog might contract them by eating raw game or rodents. Tapeworms often look like grains of rice around your dog's anus.

• Whipworms (*Trichuris vulpis*) are worms that feed off blood in the intestine. Dogs contract whipworms by eating contaminated soil.

All worms are bad news. Signs of worm infestation can include diarrhea (including bloody diarrhea), vomiting, poor haircoat, anemia, weight loss, and sometimes a garlic odor on the breath. If you suspect worms, do not treat them yourself. Not all dewormers work on all worms,

and your veterinarian is more likely to have a dewormer that is more effective than what you can buy over the counter. Bring a stool sample from your dog to your veterinarian for analysis. He can then prescribe the correct medication.

Heartworm

Heartworm is a deadly parasite your Labradoodle can contract. Heartworm is prevalent through most of the continental United States, although it is rarer in the Rocky Mountain west.

Mosquitoes transmit heartworm after feeding on an infected dog. The mosquito picks up the microfilariae or heartworm larvae, and the larvae incubate in the mosquito for several days. The mosquito then goes and feeds off another

Heartworm is a deadly parasite that can damage your dog's heart and even kill him, but there are preventatives you can buy from your veterinarian.

dog, injecting the microfilariae into another dog, thus infecting him. The heartworm larvae eventually move to the heart and lungs and even the veins in the liver. If left untreated, the dog will die from heartworm.

Treating heartworm is somewhat risky and very expensive. It is safer, more cost-effective, and certainly healthier to your Labradoodle to prevent heartworm with heartworm preventatives. The latest guideline suggests that dogs should stay on heartworm preventatives year-round and be tested yearly.

The following are the available preventatives:
• Heartgard and Heartgard Plus (Ivermectin)—Very effective at preventing heartworm. Some dogs are sensitive to it and should not be put on it, but that sensitivity is rare. Heartgard Plus controls roundworms and hookworms as well.
• Interceptor (Milnemycin)—Very effective at controlling heartworm and can be used as an alternative to ivermectin. Interceptor also controls roundworms, hookworms, and whipworms.
• Sentinel (Milbemycin and Lufenuron)—Like Interceptor, but also controls fleas
• Revolution (Selamectin)—A systemic that works as a monthly heartworm and flea preventative.

Basic Medical Skills Every Owner Needs

Occasionally you may have to take your Labradoodle's temperature or give him medication. This section shows you how to do it with minimal fuss.

Taking Your Labradoodle's Temperature

It used to be that you had to use the rectal method in taking your dog's temperature. Nowadays ear thermometers are available so that you can take your dog's temperature as fast as your doctor takes yours. However, these can be a bit pricey, and some dogs' ears don't work well with them. So, you may be stuck with taking your dog's temperature rectally.

If you must take your dog's temperature rectally, be sure to use an unbreakable electronic rectal thermometer. Wash the end thoroughly with soap and water and then rinse it with isopropyl alcohol. Use petroleum jelly (Vaseline) to lubricate it, turn it on, and wait until it is ready. Then, while holding your dog quietly, insert the end into your dog's rectum. Insert it enough so it will get a good reading, but don't force it in. Wait until the thermometer beeps before removing.

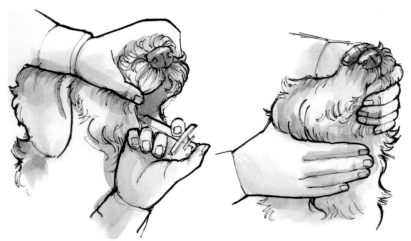

Giving a pill with the pill gun is both safe and easy.

Wipe the thermometer off with a paper towel and read it. Normal temperatures for dogs vary between 100 and 102.5°F.

Giving Your Dog a Pill

Sometimes your veterinarian may ask you to give your Labradoodle medication in pill form. Some pet owners have a tough time pilling their dogs, but it doesn't have to be that way. If your Labradoodle is bad at taking pills, ask your vet if the type of pill is available in a tasty formula (some are!).

If the pill isn't in a form your Labradoodle will like, you can try making it taste yummy by molding a bit of cheese or peanut butter (if you're not allergic to it) around the pill or by putting it in a product called Pill Pockets (ask your veterinarian about them or you can buy them from some catalogue pet supply places). Both methods make pilling easy.

But let's say this just doesn't work or the medication is to be given without food. The next step is to pick up a pet piller or pill gun from either your veterinarian or pet supply catalogue. These look remarkably like tiny syringes that hold the pill on the end. You slip the pill in the pill gun and, while holding the delivery end, slide the pill gun in your dog's mouth so the end with the pill goes to the back of the tongue. Depress the end that releases the pill. Remove the pill gun, raise your dog's muzzle with his mouth closed, and stroke his throat gently until he swallows. These are quite effective and much easier than trying to pill the old-fashioned way.

If you really want to pill the old-fashioned way, open your dog's mouth and put the pill as far back as you possibly can get it. Close your dog's mouth and raise his muzzle with his mouth closed. Stroke your dog's throat gently until he swallows.

Giving Your Dog Liquid Medicine

Your veterinarian may require you to give your Labradoodle liquid medicine. Giving your

Diarrhea and Vomiting

The most common problem many pet owners face is when their dog gets a stomach bug. If your Labradoodle throws up or has diarrhea, should you worry?

It's not necessary, but you should watch your Labradoodle carefully. Both diarrhea and vomiting can lead to dehydration, which is very dangerous. Pale and pasty gums are a sign of dehydration as is a slow response on the skin snap test. If your dog is running a fever (over 102.5°F) with the diarrhea or vomiting, you need to bring your Labradoodle to the veterinarian immediately.

Vomiting once is not necessarily a cause for concern, but if your Labradoodle projectile vomits, vomits frequently, starts becoming dehydrated, has blood or what looks like black coffee grounds in the vomit, or retches without vomiting, you must seek veterinary attention.

Diarrhea too isn't necessarily a cause for immediate concern. But bloody diarrhea, diarrhea with lots of mucus, dark tarry diarrhea, diarrhea that causes dehydration, and diarrhea that doesn't respond to medication is a concern, and you should bring your Labradoodle to the veterinarian.

In cases of mild diarrhea or vomiting, you can give your Labradoodle some pet kaolin product, which is available at pet supply stores, through catalogues, and online. Occasionally raw pumpkin or psyllium can correct mild diarrhea. Follow the dosage directions. Encourage your Labradoodle to drink water or unflavored pediatric electrolyte solution (Pedialyte). You can mix a little broth in if he doesn't like the flavor.

Withhold food for the next 24 hours and then start him on a mixture of boiled hamburger or boiled chicken and rice. Feed him several small meals instead of one or two big meals. If he does well with that, you can begin mixing his regular food back in slowly. If there is no improvement or he gets worse, take your Labradoodle to the veterinarian immediately.

dog liquid medicine is relatively easy, provided you have the proper equipment. If the medication can be given with food, see if mixing it with your Labradoodle's meal works. If he refuses to eat or must have the medication without food, there's another way to administer it that's fairly easy.

Ask your veterinarian for an oral syringe or a large syringe without a needle with the medication level marked off. Dip the end of the syringe into the medication and pull back to draw the medication into the syringe to the proper dosage. (Be careful not to let any air in—if you do, depress the syringe to put the medication back in the bottle and try again.)

Hold your Labradoodle's head and slide the tip of the syringe in the side of his mouth at the cheek. Gently push on the plunger to dispense the liquid and—while keeping his mouth closed—tilt his head up and rub his throat gently until he swallows. Be careful that your Labradoodle does not aspirate any into his lungs.

NUTRITION

In this chapter, I cover the basic diets and diet fads. What are the positive sides— and negative sides—of feeding both commercial and homemade diets.

If you ask a thousand experts what to feed your Labradoodle, you're likely to get about a thousand different responses. Make no mistake, nutrition is sort of a controversial hot topic when it comes to what to feed your dog (though it really doesn't need to be). You'll hear about commercial food, homemade diets, table scraps, and a bunch of other feeding recommendations. The question is, what's really right for your Labradoodle?

Do-It-Yourself or Store-Bought?

It used to be pretty easy to feed a dog. You opened up a bag of dog food, poured it out, and fed your dog. What could be simpler?

Feed your Labradoodle a healthy diet and he'll look beautiful.

It still can be that simple, if you're so inclined. There are plenty of good dog foods that are AAFCO (Association of American Feed Control Officials) certified and will provide all the nutrition your dog will need. You can choose a good premium food and feed your Labradoodle, and he should do just fine on it.

But what about raw diets and homemade diets? Maybe your Labradoodle's breeder or veterinarian recommends them. Or maybe a friend tells you that you must feed a raw diet or your Labradoodle will get sick. Should you feed your Labradoodle a raw diet?

Maybe, but it really depends on you and your preferences. Raw and homemade diets can be a bit more inconvenient than commercial diets. Raw diets may harbor dangerous bacteria, and diets with raw bones can be dangerous and cause intestinal perforations and blockages. Both raw and homemade diets may not be complete and balanced. On the other hand,

Exercise is healthy for your dog, too!

you know what your Labradoodle is eating, and many homemade and raw enthusiasts swear that their dogs are healthier on these diets.

The results are, at best, inconclusive. There are many dogs who live long and healthy lives on commercial diets (my own dogs have lived to 18 years old, on occasion), and many dogs who thrive on raw and homemade diets. In the end, it's really a matter of preference.

This chapter covers primarily store-bought food, but it does include a section on raw and homemade diets at the end, for those interested in them.

If you choose to buy commercial food instead of preparing it yourself, be certain that the dog food states on the package that it meets or

exceeds the guidelines set forth by AAFCO and that it is complete and balanced. Not all dog food is, so look at the label first. What AAFCO certification says is that the dog food is formulated to the guideline as set forth by AAFCO or has proven that the dog food can sustain a dog in a 6-week feeding trial according to AAFCO guidelines. Even though this may not be the end-all for nutrition, for some owners commercial dog food that meet AAFCO guidelines is in general a good step toward maintaining a healthy Labradoodle.

Premium Dog Food Versus Generic

Let's say you've decided that you wish to feed a commercial dog food. You like the idea that it's convenient and it's less likely to spoil than a homemade diet. But what dog foods are best for your Labradoodle. You've probably heard a lot of hype about premium dog food— and I'll recommend it too, with some caveats. My definition of premium does not always match a dog food manufacturer's definition of premium, largely because, at this time, there is no AAFCO definition for premium dog food. Premium is largely a marketing term, so keep this in mind when you're shopping for dog food.

In my mind, a truly premium dog food is one that is more than an 85 percent digestibe. That means that 85 percent or more of the dog food can be used by your Labradoodle and won't come out the other end as feces. This means you feed less to obtain the same result—it's nutrient-packed, and your dog has smaller stools and more energy. Some grocery-store-type dog foods (although some premium foods

But My Dog Hates It

Many pet owners buy some of the best food, only to find that their dog won't eat it. Like people, dogs have different tastes, and what tastes good to a million dogs may not taste good to yours. All the nutrition in the world isn't doing a bit of good if you can't get your dog to eat it.

So, what do you do? You can find a premium dog food that your Labradoodle likes and feed him that. Or you can use some of those special flavor enhancer sauces that will make his food taste better. Or, you can mix canned and dry.

have shown up in grocery stores, hence the change in name), which I often call "generic" foods, have fillers and indigestible matter in them, requiring you to feed as much as five times more food to obtain the same nutrition. These bargain foods are often no bargain, and you end up paying the same amount because you have to feed so much. What's more, the protein isn't necessarily from a good source, so your Labradoodle doesn't really get as much protein as he needs.

So, you need to feed a premium dog food and not a generic dog food. But if premium is a marketing term, how do you tell if the food is any good? First of all, it must be AAFCO certified. This is absolutely essential; otherwise, the food will have imbalances.

Second, look at the ingredient label. Ingredients are listed from the most ingredients to the least. The first ingredients should be a meat protein source such as beef, chicken, fish, poultry, meat, or some kind of by-product. (By-

products aren't bad as we'll see later). If the first ingredients are plant-based or if the first ingredient is meat followed by several types of plant materials as the second through fourth ingredients, the food is more grain-based than meat-based. A dog food that has chicken, poultry by-product meal, rice, and fat is a better food than one that has chicken, corn, fat and rice as the first four ingredients.

Third, the dog food should be highly digestible. Almost every so-called premium dog food will say it's highly digestible, but the key to learning whether it really is, is to contact the dog food company and ask what percentage of the food is digestible. (It's unlikely that information will be on the package.) A dog food that is 85 percent or more digestible is a premium dog food. Anything less isn't premium.

Deciphering the Label

Pet food is regulated both at the federal government level and at the state level. At the federal level the Food and Drug Administration's Center for Veterinary Medicine (CVM) regulates pet foods and their labeling.

A dog food label has several parts to it. These include:

✔ The Product Name—Includes company and the type of food, usually.

✔ Net Quantity Statement—How much food is in the bag or can.

✔ Manufacturer's Name and Address—Who made it and how to contact them.

✔ Ingredient List—What's in the dog food. (I discuss that in the above section on "Premium Dog Food Versus Generic.")

✔ Guaranteed Analysis—The basic nutrition in the dog food.

Your Labradoodle should like his food, too. Find something he'll enjoy eating.

✔ Nutritional Adequacy Statement—A statement that the dog food is either complete and balanced or not.

✔ Feeding directions—How to feed the dog food.

We'll look at the most important parts of the label: the Product Name, the Guaranteed Analysis, and the Nutritional Adequacy Statement.

Product Name

The product name of the food usually has the manufacturer's name in it, but this is not required. Depending on what the name is,

you can sometimes decipher the amount of ingredients.

• If a meat source is identified without any modifiers, such as *Chicken for Dogs*, chicken must make up 95% of the weight of the ingredients. However, this does not extend to grains, so *Lamb and Rice for Dogs* must have 95% lamb. (If water is added, at least 70% of the weight of the food must be the protein.) Also, if there are two types of meat, as in *Beef and Lamb for Dogs*, beef and lamb together must make up 95%.

• If the food has the words "dinner" or "formula," such as *Beef Dinner for Dogs*, beef must comprise at least 25% of the weight. Unlike the 95% rule, if the food says something like *Lamb and Rice Formula*, the two ingredients must make up 25% of the total weight.

• If the dog food has the word "with," it means that 3% of the food has that item, so *Dog Food with Beef* would only have 3% beef (as opposed to *Beef Dog Food*, which would be 95% beef).

Be sure the dog food you buy has an AAFCO nutrition adequacy statement to ensure a beautiful and healthy pet.

Guaranteed Analysis

All dog food must have a minimum *guaranteed analysis,* that is the minimal percentages of crude protein and crude fat and the maximum percentages of fiber and moisture provided by the dog food on a by-weight basis. In terms of nutritional content, it's difficult to compare canned food and dry food because of the moisture content, but you can usually compare like foods, such as dry food to dry food and canned to canned.

Dog foods must have a minimum of 18% protein/5% fat for adult foods on a dry matter basis (without water) and 22% protein/8% fat for puppy foods (on a dry matter basis) to meet standards set for by the American Association of Feed Control Officials (AAFCO). More on AAFCO later in this chapter.

If you're interested in learning how to compare nutrition in dog foods, check out my book *The Complete Idiot's Guide to Dog Health and Nutrition* with James M. Wingert DVM, Alpha Books, 2003.

Nutrition Adequacy Statement

All dog foods that claim to be "complete and balanced" must have an AAFCO nutritional adequacy statement for "growth" or "all life stages" for puppies or "maintenance" or "all life stages" for adult dogs. These statements read either "*Product* is formulated to meet the nutritional levels established by the AAFCO Dog Food Nutrient Profiles" or "Animal feeding tests using AAFCO procedures substantiate that *product* provides complete and balanced nutrition." Without either of these statements, the dog food cannot be considered complete and balanced—and therefore should not be used as your dog's main source of nutrition.

Types of Dog Food: Dry, Canned, Semi-Moist, Frozen, or Freeze-Dried?

There's a variety of dog foods on the market, and not just brands. Dog food comes in different forms including dry, canned, semi-moist, frozen, and freeze-dried. Let's look at each of them.

✔ Dry food is the most readily available and is often in various choices such as growth (puppy), adult, performance, lite, senior, and other types (large breed, small breed, etc.). It's usually offered in various flavors such as beef, chicken, or lamb. It's also the most cost-effective because it's cheaper than any other type of food. Dry food is usually good from 6 months to a year. The downside of dry food is that it may be less palatable than other forms of foods.

✔ Canned food is the second most common type of food. It's highly palatable and usually comes in flavors. It has a good shelf life (more than a year). The downside to canned food is that you must feed more in order to get the same nutrition as dry dog food; thus, it is more expensive. You pay a lot more for processing, canning, and water weight than you would for a bag of dog food. Most people like mixing canned food in with dry to make the dry more palatable.

✔ Semi-moist dog food is usually in those little burger shapes and look like hamburger. They're somewhat expensive and chock-full of sugar, artificial colors, and flavors to remain soft and look pleasing to people.

✔ Compressed meat rolls, which look like salamis, are another type of food that could be considered semi-moist. These meat rolls are *not* the same as semi-moist food. Instead, many are all-natural rolls that are semi-dehydrated meat

mixed with other ingredients to make them complete and balanced. They're highly palatable, but they can be expensive when compared to dry food.

✔ Frozen food is often the answer to the raw diet feeders. This food is highly palatable and often is made from human-grade ingredients. Dogs love this food, and it can be the number one choice for picky eaters. However, it can be difficult to get in some areas, and not all pet supply stores will carry it because it requires a freezer case. Likewise, you will need some extra freezer space, especially if you're feeding several dogs. This is an expensive option because you're paying for water weight in the food and also freezer storage. An outage could be a very costly if you feed this type of food.

✔ Freeze-dried food is nother type of food being offered. It is often made by the manufacturers of frozen food for people who wish to feed their dogs while on a trip or when they need added convenience. This food has a good shelf life (6 months to a year) and is convenient to feed. It's highly palatable but is very expensive because of the dehydration process.

What's the best food for your Labradoodle? It really depends on what you're looking for. For convenience and cost, dry dog food is probably the best. For palatability, canned food, com-

Feed an adult Labradoodle twice a day.

pressed meat rolls, and frozen and dehydrated dog food all work really well.

Free-Feeding

Lots of people free-feed, that is, put the dog food in the bowl and leave it out for their dog all day. People do this mostly because they don't think they have the time to feed their dogs, however, there are plenty of good reasons not to free-feed.

Why shouldn't you free-feed? You won't know how much your Labradoodle is really eating if you free-feed. You can't control his portions when you free-feed, and your Labradoodle may become a bit pudgy—or *a lot* pudgy.

Another reason is that often a dog not eating is the first sign of an illness. If you free-feed, you never know when your Labradoodle skips a meal or if he is really having a problem.

Certain dog food, such as canned, fresh, and frozen can quickly become full of bacteria and spoiled if left out long. Even dry dog food can become stale and less appetizing if left outside the bag.

Lastly, it's hard to train a dog who has been free-fed. In clicker training (and other forms of positive training), you're trying to get your dog enthusiastic about the training. The food reward isn't exciting if you've stuffed yourself throughout the day.

Feeding a dog takes a few seconds to prepare, especially if it's dry food. By measuring your dog's food out and giving it to him at certain times of the day, you can ensure that your

Labradoodle will be getting the right nutrition. You'll also know if he's not feeling well because he may not eat his food.

How to Feed

One size does not fit all when it comes to feeding your Labradoodle. How you feed your Labradoodle will depend largely on his age, his activity level, and the type of dog food you feed him. You want to feed him enough to keep him at a healthy weight—neither too fat nor too thin.

But how much is just right? There should be feeding guidelines on the bag or can of dog food—that's usually a good place to start. But realize that most commercial dog food guidelines err a bit on the heavy side, so if your

Labradoodle starts getting fat, you'll need to reduce the portions.

Obesity

Like people, dogs can and do get fat. It doesn't take much, really. Most dogs have owners who hand out lots of big, fatty treats.

Your Labradoodle is a healthy weight if you can easily feel his ribs, hipbones, and spine without his bones protruding. If he has so much padding that he feels ribless (or nearly ribless), you should consult your veterinarian for a proper diet and exercise program to reduce his weight.

Hypoallergenic Diets

Some dogs are allergic to certain ingredients in their food. If you suspect that your Labradoodle is allergic to something in his food, talk with your veterinarian. Your veterinarian may want to put your Labradoodle on a hypoallergenic diet with a novel protein source (one not usually found in dog food such as venison, duck, or kangaroo) and an uncommon carbohydrate (potatoes or barley).

If you suspect your Labradoodle has food allergies, don't try to diagnose the allergies yourself. Foods such as lamb and rice mixes used to be hypoallergenic, but they are no longer because these foods have been used in many different pet foods. Your veterinarian will know what diet to try and will give specific instructions on how to feed your Labradoodle.

Treats

There are plenty of dog treats on the market, but many of them are high in calories, salt, and

═══ T I P ═══

Prevent Bloat During Feeding

Bloat is a life-threatening condition where the stomach fills with gas and fluid. In severe cases, the stomach actually twists on its axis, shutting off both the lower esophagus and intestine. In this case, the dog goes into shock and dies a very painful death. If your Labradoodle begins to show signs of bloat, *get emergency veterinary attention immediately!* Signs include swelling of the abdomen, retching without vomiting, drooling, restlessness, pacing, panting, straining to defecate, pain, and obvious discomfort.

Bloat occurs most often in deep-chested breeds, so a standard-sized Labradoodle can be affected. It occurs more often in males than females and most often in dogs older than two years old. Bloat usually occurs right after feeding, but it can take up to three hours to occur.

You can help prevent bloat.

• If your Labradoodle is a fast eater, you may want to moisten his food to help slow his eating.

• Adding water to his food will help the food evacuate from his stomach much faster.

• Feeding several small meals throughout the day, instead of one or two large meals, also reduces the risk.

• Don't feed and leave. Watch for signs of gastric distress or the stomach becoming enlarged.

• Don't switch foods, add table scraps, or feed old or rancid food. This can cause stomach upsets that lead to bloat.

sugar and low in nutritional value. If you buy prepackaged treats, try to find those that are low in fat, sugar, and salt and that have no artificial colors or flavors. I regularly use tiny bits of compressed meat rolls made for dog food as treats.

You can help keep your Labradoodle healthy by providing him with small, healthy snacks. These include carrots, celery, lettuce hearts, cabbage pieces (I have one dog who loves Bok Choy), and tiny bits of apple. Avoid onions, grapes, raisins, chocolate, and macadamia nuts because they are poisonous to dogs. Bits of lean, cooked meat diced in tiny portions also make good treats.

If You Want to Do a Homemade Diet

Homemade diets (including feeding raw) are very popular because dogs love them, and owners can monitor the quality of food they're feeding their dogs. There's no doubt that many dogs are thriving on these diets, but whether they're as good or better than commercial diets is arguable.

The difficulty with these diets is that, in most instances, many don't meet the basic AAFCO guidelines to maintain a healthy dog. If not analyzed by a veterinary nutritionist, these diets may have critical imbalances that commercial food does not. Likewise, raw diets often have dangerous bacteria such as *E. coli*, salmonella, and campylobacter, which can be dangerous to young puppies and older dogs. Even in reasonably healthy dogs, these bacteria can pose a problem and can be transmitted to you. Certain diets tell you that you need to feed raw bones, but bones can be very dangerous and can cause blockages and perforated intestines.

Good nutrition will help your Labradoodle live a long and healthy life.

The positive side to homemade meals is that you know what is in them. If your Labradoodle has allergies to certain ingredients, you can easily by-pass those ingredients. Homemade meals tend to be extremely palatable because they're fresh. And if you formulate them right, they're very healthy.

If this is something you want to do, you'll need to do a fair amount of research on dog nutrition—and not just the hype that many raw food proponents write up. Avoid internet information unless it comes from a reputable source such as a veterinary college. Talk to veterinary nutritionists to formulate the best possible food for your Labradoodle. And when you design the right diet for your Labradoodle, get it analyzed by a veterinary college. It'll be somewhat expensive up front, but once you do, you'll know you're feeding your Labradoodle a complete and balanced diet.

GROOMING THE LABRADOODLE

A clean, sweet-smelling Labradoodle is a pleasure to own. A stinky Labradoodle is, well, a dirty dog. In this chapter, we cover the basics for keeping your Labradoodle clean and sweet-smelling.

Types of Coats

Because the Labradoodle is a blending of two breeds, you may or may not get the type of coat you want. Basically, there are three types of recognized coats on an Australian Labradoodle: fleece, wool, and haircoat. The fleece and wool coats shed little, but the hair coat will shed in various degrees. More early generation dogs will have haircoats.

Looking for a Professional Groomer

Many Labradoodle owners, when faced with clipping and keeping a Labradoodle coat in tip-top shape, decide that maybe a professional groomer isn't such a bad idea. Professional groomers can be a bit pricey, charging anywhere from $35 to $75 for a complete groom-

Labradoodles have many types of coats. Which one does yours have?

ing; however, prices vary largely on the condition of the dog's coat, where you live, and what services need to be performed. For example, a quick bath, brush, and touch-up clip will be cheaper than a total dematting and show cut on top of the bath and clip. Prices are naturally going to be lower in certain areas such as the South or parts of the Midwest than in Chicago, Boston, or New York City.

Looking for a professional groomer doesn't have to be daunting. Try the following to find the right groomer:

✔ Ask other dog-owning friends who they use.

✔ Ask your veterinarian if he or she has recommendations. Often a veterinarian has an on-site groomer.

✔ Ask your dog trainer or your dog's breeder. Sometimes he or she can recommend a groomer in the area.

✔ Look in the groomer directory at *www.findagroomer.com.*

Common tools: nail grinder, ear and cotton swabs, slicker brush, styptic powder, toothbrush and toothpaste, nail clippers, shears, pin brush, and comb.

When you find a few groomers you're interested in, make an appointment to visit the groomer to meet them and find out what services they perform. Most groomers will clip nails, clean ears, empty anal sacs, bathe, brush, and clip, but don't assume they will. Ask the groomer what they will do for your Labradoodle.

When visiting the groomer, you should see a fairly well-organized shop that's maintained well. If it's busy, you may see water and hair on the floor, but you shouldn't get the impression that it's totally chaotic, understaffed, or filthy. Watch how the groomer cares for the animals. The groomer should be gentle and interested in the animals' comfort.

Grooming Equipment

Regardless of whether you groom your Labradoodle yourself or whether you take him to a groomer, you're still going to need to groom your Labradoodle—if only for touch-ups. You're

---

TIP

If You Slip Up

What do you do if you make a mistake? If it's not harmful to your Labradoodle, you can try to fix it by blending in the fur. If that doesn't work, you may need to have a professional groomer fix the problem.

If you injure your Labradoodle, bring him to the veterinarian at once.

---

going to need some basic equipment and supplies to keep your Labradoodle looking his best:

✔ Slicker brush
✔ Metal comb
✔ Mat rake
✔ Flea comb
✔ Grooming table
✔ Nail clippers for dogs or nail grinder
✔ Shampoo and conditioner pH balanced for dogs
✔ Detangler spray
✔ Toothbrush and toothpaste for dogs
✔ Tweezers or forceps
✔ Clippers with size 30 and 10 blades and snap-on combs for appropriate length
✔ Cooling spray and lubricant for clippers
✔ Styptic powder or nail cauterizer
✔ Otic solution
✔ Ear powder

These are the bare minimum requirements for grooming your dog. You'll also want to have towels (both paper and bath towels), cotton balls, and cotton swabs. You can purchase these items online over the internet, from pet supply catalogues, or from pet supply stores.

Your Labradoodle will look great coming back from the groomers.

When Should You Groom?

How often you should groom depends largely on how often your Labradoodle gets dirty and how often he needs a touch-up on his coat. It's a good idea to brush and comb your Labradoodle at least twice a week and to bathe and clip him once a month to keep him looking good. If the shampoo and conditioner is pH balanced for a dog's coat, you can do this more often, especially if he gets muddy. These shampoos and conditioners won't dry out the coat like shampoos that aren't pH balanced.

Dental Care

Caring for your Labradoodle's teeth is vitally important. Dogs seldom get cavities, but they do get gingivitis and gum disease, as well as plaque and tartar to accumulate on the teeth. In advanced stages, your Labradoodle can actually lose his teeth and have painful abscesses, which can seriously affect your Labradoodle's health. So, dental care is very important for your Labradoodle.

TIP

No Tranquilizers!

If at all possible, avoid groomers who tranquilize dogs. Some tranquilizers can cause seizure-prone dogs to go into convulsions.

Brushing Your Labradoodle's Teeth

One of the ways to keep your Labradoodle's teeth clean and his breath kissably sweet is to brush his teeth every day. You can do this with a toothbrush and toothpaste made for dogs, which is usually beef, chicken, or malt flavored. When you brush his teeth, you need to brush all surfaces, just like you would a person's, only he doesn't have to rinse and spit.

Getting your Labradoodle used to brushing his teeth may take a bit of time, especially if your Labradoodle doesn't like having his mouth handled. Here's the way to get your Labradoodle used to having his teeth brushed:

1. Get your Labradoodle used to you touching his mouth by gently touching his lips and gently flipping up his lips to expose his teeth.

2. Once he's used to this, get a washcloth and wet it with warm water. Take the corner and gently massage your Labradoodle's gums and teeth for a few seconds with the washcloth.

3. When your Labradoodle tolerates this, purchase some finger brushes (available at a pet supply store) and put some pet toothpaste on it and try brushing your Labradoodle's teeth with it.

4. Eventually, your Labradoodle will accept the brushing, especially if you get him slowly used to it.

Stylin' in my new 'do.

Spotting a Dental Problem

Just like people, dogs can have dental problems. Here are some basic signs that it's time for a trip to the doggie dentist:

• Bad breath or "doggie breath." Dogs don't naturally have bad breath. If your Labradoodle does, it's a sign he needs to have his teeth examined.

• Refusal to eat or picky eating habits. Lack of appetite may signal a dental problem.

Sudden unexplained chewing. Puppies often chew while teething to relieve pain. Adults too can suddenly start chewing if their teeth hurt them.

• Sudden aggressiveness. A toothache can make anyone cranky.

• Red, swollen gums.

• Teeth with an accumulation of tartar on them.

• Lump above or below a tooth. They could indicate an abscess.

• Lumps or bumps in the mouth that aren't normal. They could be the sign of tumors or oral cancer.

• Pawing at the face or mouth.

• Drippy or runny nose.

Keeping Your Dog's Ears Clean

The Labradoodle is particularly susceptible to ear problems, especially if you don't keep them clean. Labradoodle's ears should be clean a sweet-smelling. If not, it's time for a trip to the veterinarian.

You can keep your Labradoodle's ears clean by cleaning them once a week with a mild otic solution made for dogs. Do not use solutions with insecticides because these can irritate your Labradoodle's sensitive ears. Here's how to clean your Labradoodle's ears:

1. Read the directions on the otic solution and squeeze the recommended amount into your Labradoodle's ear.

2. Gently massage the ear.

3. Use gauze or cotton balls and wipe the ear dry.

4. Repeat steps 1–3 on the other ear.

Many Labradoodles have what is called "Poodle ear"; that is, the ears have tufts of hair growing out of the ear canals. These tufts collect bacteria, dirt, and other gunk and should be removed. This involves plucking the ear hair out. Many groomers use ear powder to facilitate plucking, but it's best if you have a professional groomer or your Labradoodle's breeder show you how it's done correctly to minimize pain. If you're squeamish or worried about getting bit, find a professional groomer to remove the ear hair.

Fleas, Ticks, and Mites

A number of external parasites can make your Labradoodle miserable. These include fleas, ticks, and mites. Fleas and ticks are especially worrisome because not only are they pests, but they can also carry some downright dangerous diseases that both you and your Labradoodle can contract. As the old saying goes, an ounce of prevention is worth a pound of cure—and with these critters, preventing them from attacking your Labradoodle will make him a happy and healthy dog.

This is probably your Labradoodle's idea of a bath. Unfortunately it can cause mats and tangles.

TIP

Mat Removal

Never, ever use scissors to cut out a mat. You can seriously injure your Labradoodle. If you must cut a mat, use the clippers. If your Labradoodle is severely matted, seek professional help.

Flea Prevention

Once fighting fleas was a lot like wholesale chemical warfare. You had to dip your dog, put flea powders and stuff on him, turn on the ultrasound traps (which never worked), put flea collars on your dog (which also didn't work),

and flea bomb your entire house. Guess what? Those days are pretty much gone.

The reason is because technology has advanced to a point where a pill or a topical liquid can kill fleas and prevent them from growing and reproducing. These flea control substances are called systemics because they are absorbed in the system of the dog and make him lethal to fleas for at least a month.

The best place to get a systemic is from your veterinarian. He or she will know just the right one to control fleas on your Labradoodle. You can buy these systemics from pet supply houses, but be careful. A few years ago, a well-known systemic was forged and sold to some internet suppliers. When in doubt, buy from your veterinarian.

If you need to get rid of fleas in the house, you may wish to ask your veterinarian what safe flea products he or she would recommend. Be sure to follow the directions on the package.

Tick Prevention

Ticks are other nasty critters. Like fleas, they can carry a host of unpleasant diseases and are very pesky. Many systemics work against ticks as well as fleas, but not all, so be sure to ask your veterinarian if the systemic your dog is on handles ticks.

There is a tick collar called Preventic that's available through veterinarians and some pet supply houses that works well. Consult your veterinarian before using any tick product.

If you find a tick on your Labradoodle, you need to remove it right away. Use tweezers or forceps, and grasp the tick close to your Labradoodle's skin and pull straight out. (You can apply a flea and tick powder recommended by your veterinarian to loosen the tick.) Don't

used alcohol, match heads, burning cigarettes, or anything like that to try to force the tick out—these items can hurt your Labradoodle or cause the tick to embed deeper.

When you pull the tick out, drop it in a sealed jar or rubbing alcohol and take to you vet for possible identification. Don't handle the tick, and wash your hands afterwards to avoid contracting any diseases. Wash the area where the tick was with soap and water, and keep an eye out for rashes or infection. If you see a rash or an infection, consult a veterinarian.

Mites

Mites are little bloodsuckers related to both ticks and spiders. There are several types of mites including:
• Ear mites—itchy ears, with red, waxy build-up and head shaking.
• Cheyletiella mange (walking dandruff)—itchy with reddish or white dandruff that seems to move (hence the name). Highly contagious to dogs and people.
• Chiggers—itchy red bumps. Keep your Labradoodle out of high grasses and away from rotting vegetation. Your veterinarian may recommend special shampoos and medication.
• Demodectic mange—loss of hair, either localized or throughout the body. Needs veterinary treatment.
• Sarcoptic mange (scabies)—severe itching, hair loss, and crusty, itchy skin. Needs veterinary treatment. Highly contagious to dogs and people.

In almost all cases, you'll need to consult with a veterinarian concerning how to get rid of the mange. Avoid over-the-counter remedies because these may have little or no effect on certain types of mites.

A healthy and happy Labradoodle.

Your Labradoodle will be healthy and look and feel better when clean and brushed. Depending on the type of coat, Labradoodles can have coats similar to Poodles or coats similar to Labrador Retrievers, or something in the middle. Not all Labradoodles have single coats and many do shed, so it's a good idea to brush and comb your Labradoodle often.

Brushing and Combing

Your Labradoodle will need to be brushed and combed a minimum of twice a week—more often if he sheds or when he is an adolescent. Start by taking a slicker brush and brush through his coat. If he's not clipped close, try back brushing,

Be sure when cutting the toenails to avoid cutting the quick.

that is, brushing against the lay of the hair, and then brush it so it lays correctly. Do this again with the comb. Lastly, if his fur isn't too thick, use a flea comb to search for fleas and to keep mats from forming.

If you find a mat, you'll have to remove it. Some groomers recommend trying to take a mat out with a slicker brush, but it is time-consuming and not always successful. The best way to take out a mat is to spray the mat with detangler solution and work your fingers through the mat so the stuff gets into the mat. Then, take your mat rake and gently rake through it (the sharp teeth should cut through the mat). If the mat is bad, you may have to resort to using electronic clippers on the mat, and gently shaving the mat away. *Never* use scissors on a mat because you can hurt your Labradoodle.

If your Labradoodle is severely matted, bring him to your veterinarian or a professional groomer. Chances are that they may have to shave your Labradoodle, but it's more healthy that dealing with a matted coat.

Bathing

This may sound odd, but you should never bathe a dirty

Labradoodle without brushing him out first. There are several good reasons for it, but basically, it's to keep your Labradoodle's coat from tangling up. It also removes a good portion of the dirt in his coat. Do the following:

• Thoroughly brush out your Labradoodle and remove all mats.

• Pour tepid water in the bathtub. Have a pH-balanced shampoo and conditioner for dogs ready. If your Labradoodle is agitated, you may wish to use a bathing noose. (*Caution*: Never leave a dog alone in a bathing noose for any reason.)

• Put your Labradoodle in the tub and soak him down. Wash him with the shampoo and rinse thoroughly.

• Apply conditioner and rinse thoroughly. You must remove all traces of the shampoo and conditioner because they will collect dirt.

• Dry your Labradoodle with towels and keep him in a warm, draft-free place until he dries. You can use a forced-air dryer made for dogs or a human hairdryer with the setting on NO HEAT. (Never use heat to dry your dog.)

• Brush and comb out your Labradoodle again.

LABRADOODLE

Clipping

Regardless of the type of coat, your Labradoodle will look good being clipped in a simple style. Most pet owners opt for the Teddy Bear clip or the pet clip because it's easy to maintain and looks good on their dogs.

If keeping your Labradoodle clipped looks particularly daunting, consider having a groomer do this about once a month to keep your Labradoodle looking good. You can also have the groomer get your Labradoodle into the right clip and then just maintain it. It's a lot easier than trying to learn the whole thing yourself.

To start clipping your Labradoodle into a Teddy Bear cut, you'll need a good set of electric clippers with size 30 and 10 blades (Oster blades) for clipping as well as an assortment of snap-on combs. These combs are for novices who want to cut their dog's coat a particular length, but who aren't necessarily good at eyeballing it. So, to clip your Labradoodle, do the following:

- With a size 10 blade, clip the underside of your Labradoodle, being careful around the anus and sex organs. This will keep him cleaner.
- Clean the blade and then with a size 10 blade, trim along the ears and follow the line of the ear flap, thus outlineing the ears.
- Change blades to a size 30 blade and use a snap-on comb with the appropriate length. (Remember, shorter coats are easier to maintain). With the snap-on comb to guide you, run the clippers all over your Labradoodle's body until the coat is even.
- Be sure to cool the blade down occasionally with clipper cooling spray. You don't want to burn your Labradoodle while clipping him.

The Teddy Bear cut.

Clipping Your Labradoodle's Toenails

Your Labradoodle's toenails need to be trimmed once a week. Depending on the color of the toenail, you must look for the quick, that is, the spongy part of the nail that supplies blood to the nail. If your Labradoodle's nails are light colored, you can see the quick as the pink part beneath the nail. You can trim up to the quick, but do not cut it, because cutting it is very painful and it will bleed profusely.

If your Labradoodle has dark nails, you'll have to make a guess where to trim. Many scissors-type nail trimmers have a safety guide that may aid you in cutting your Labradoodle's nails safely. If at any time, the nail feels spongy, stop. When in doubt, have a professional groomer or veterinarian cut them.

Have a nail cauterizer or styptic powder on hand in case you accidentally cut the quick. Both will prevent bleeding if used according to directions.

Lastly, many dogs who hate nail clippers can tolerate nail grinders. The same care needs to be taken to not nick the quick because, in extreme cases, it can cause an infection.

Organizations

Agility Association of Canada (AAC)
RR #2
Lucan, Ontario N0N2J0
(519) 657-7636

AKC Companion Animal Recovery
5580 Centerview Drive, Suite 250
Raleigh, NC 27606-3389
(800) 252-7894
www.akccar.org

American Kennel Club (AKC)
5580 Centerview Drive
Raleigh, NC 27606-3390
(919) 233-9767
www.akc.org

Association of Pet Dog Trainers
150 Executive Center Drive, Box 35
Greenville, SC 29615
(800) PET-DOGS (800-738-3647)
www.apdt.com

Australian Labradoodle Association
  of America (ALAA)
http://www.ilainc.com/index.html

Canine Eye Registration Foundation (CERF)
Department of Veterinary Clinical Science
School of Veterinary Medicine
Purdue University
West Lafayette, IN 47907
(765) 494-8179
Fax: (765) 494-9981
www.vet.purdue.edu/~yshen/cerf.html/

International Australian Labradoodle Association
http://www.ilainc.com/IALA/index.html

National Association of Professional Pet Sitters
15000 Commerce Parkway, Suite C
Mt. Laurel, New Jersey 08054
(856) 439-0324
Fax: (856) 439-0525
www.petsitters.org

North American Flyball Association, Inc.
1400 W. Devon Avenue, #512
Chicago, IL 60660
(309) 688-9840
www.flyballdogs.com/flyball.html

Don't be fooled by claims of hypoallergenic dogs or shedless dogs—there's no such thing as a hypoallergenic dog and many Labradoodles can shed.

You should request a contract for either a puppy or an adult. Be sure you understand the contract or have a lawyer look it over.

Orthopedic Foundation for Animals (OFA)
2300 Nifong Boulevard
Columbia, MO 65201
(573) 442-0418
www.offa.org

PennHIP
Synbiotics Corporation
11011 Via Frontera
San Diego, CA 92127
(858) 451-3771
Fax: (858) 451-5719
www.synbiotics.com/html/chdpennhip.html

Pet Sitters International
201 East King Street
King, NC 27021-9161
(336) 983-9222
Fax: (336) 983-5266
www.petsit.com

United Kennel Club (UKC)
100 East Kilgore Road
Kalamazoo, MI 49001-5593
www.ukcdogs.com

United States Dog Agility Association
   (USDAA)
P.O. Box 850955
Richardson, TX 75085-0955
(972) 231-9700
Information Line: 1-888-AGILITY
www.usdaa.com
E-mail: info@usdaa.com

Labradoodles can be loyal friends.

About the Author

Margaret H. Bonham is a six-time award-winning pet, science fiction, and fantasy author of 22 books, including *Introduction to Dog Agility, A Dog's Wisdom,* and *Dog Grooming for Dummies.* She is a world-renowned pet expert, trainer, and behaviorist featured in *USA Today Weekend, Prevention* magazine, *Animal Planet Radio, Pet Central,* and various radio and newspaper articles.

Dedication

In memory of my mother, Betty Holowinski (August 7, 1927–December 28, 2006). And for Larry, who's always there.

Acknowledgments

Special thanks go to Jessica Faust at BookEnds, Acquisitions Editor Wayne Barr, Editor Anthony Regolino, and Caroline Coile.

A Note on Pronouns

Throughout this book, the pronoun "he" has been used when referring to the animal. No gender bias is intended by this writing style.

Important Note

This pet owner's manual tells the reader how to buy or adopt and care for a Labradoodle. The author and the publisher consider it important to point out that the advice given in the book is meant primarily for normally developed dogs of excellent physical health and sound temperament.

Anyone who acquires a fully-grown dog should be aware that the animal has already formed its basic impressions of human beings. The new owner should observe the animal carefully, including its behavior toward humans, and, whenever possible, should meet the previous owner.

Caution is further advised in the association of children with dogs, in meeting with other dogs, and in exercising the dog without a leash.

Even well-behaved and carefully supervised dogs can sometimes damage property or cause accidents. It is therefore in the owner's interest to be adequately insured against such eventualities, and we strongly urge all dog owners to purchase a liability policy that also covers their dog.

Photo Credits

Barbara Augello: 4, 32, 52, 62, 89, and 93 (bottom); Norvia Behling: 6 (top), 10 (top and bottom), 19, 56, and 79; Kent Dannen: 8, 14, 17, 41, 44, 69, and 74; Tara Darling: 6 (bottom), 9, 11, 16 (top and bottom), 18, 21, 23, 25, 26, 29, 30, 36, 53, 54, 61, 76, 86, and 93 (top); Jean M. Fogle: 42, 43 (left and right), 45, 46, 47 (left and right), 48, 49 (left, right top, and right bottom), 50, 66, and 87; Pamela E. McCarl of Eden Valley Manor: 2–3, 5, 13, 20, 31, 64, 65, 67, 68, 77, 81, 83, 85, and 92; and Connie Summers: 7, 12, 22, 24, 27, 28, 33, 34, 40, 72, 73, and 82.

Cover Photos

Front cover: Connie Summers; back cover: Jean M. Fogle; inside front cover: Tara Darling; inside back cover: Kent Dannen.

All inquiries should be addressed to:
Barron's Educational Series, Inc.
250 Wireless Boulevard
Hauppauge, NY 11788
www.barronseduc.com

ISBN-13: 978-0-7641-3698-6
ISBN-10: 0-7641-3698-4

Library of Congress Catalog Card No. 2006037864

Library of Congress Cataloging-in-Publication Data
Bonham, Margaret H.
    Labradoodles : everything about purchase, care, nutrition, behavior, and training / Margaret H. Bonham.
        p. cm. — (A complete pet owners manual)
    Includes index.
    ISBN-13: 978-0-7641-3698-6
    ISBN-10: 0-7641-3698-4
    1. Labradoodle. I. Title.

SF429.L29B66   2007
636.72—dc22   2006037864

Printed in China
9 8 7 6